Y0-BSX-901

RETURN
and
SUCCEED

12 Powerful Habits *for*
Success after Your Mission

ROBERT R. SHALLENBERGER

Covenant Communications, Inc.

Cover designed by Dawn Teagarden
Cover design copyright © 2016 by Covenant Communications, Inc.
Published by Covenant Communications, Inc.
American Fork, Utah

Copyright © 2016 by Robert R. Shallenberger
All rights reserved. No part of this book may be reproduced in any format or in any medium without the written permission of the publisher, Covenant Communications, Inc., P.O. Box 416, American Fork, UT 84003. This work is not an official publication of The Church of Jesus Christ of Latter-day Saints. The views expressed within this work are the sole responsibility of the author and do not necessarily reflect the position of The Church of Jesus Christ of Latter-day Saints, Covenant Communications, Inc., or any other entity.

Printed in the United States of America
First Printing: January 2016

22 21 20 19 18 17 16   10 9 8 7 6 5 4 3 2 1

ISBN 978-1-68047-366-7

CONTENTS

ACKNOWLEDGMENTS

I AM DEEPLY GRATEFUL TO so many who have helped make this book possible. There are countless people who have shaped my life and taught me how to become a better person than I would have otherwise been. As I reflect on my life, there is a long list of people who have deeply influenced me.

I'm always hesitant to list names because it will certainly exclude many people who have been influential in my life. However, I would be remiss to not include a few names here.

Tonya Shallenberger—a tremendous wife and example. She is an unbelievable person who has contributed so many ideas and tireless support in all our adventures!

Steve and Roxanne Shallenberger—my parents are the ones who stuck with me through all the years. They continue to inspire, mentor, and teach me what love and charity really look like.

Robbie, Bella, Lana, and Clara—my children are the reason for doing so many of the things I do. They amaze me with their imagination, hard work, fun personalities, and laughter.

David, Steven, Tommy, Daniel, and Anne—I certainly wouldn't be the same without four amazing brothers and an off-the-chart sister! Each of them has shaped my life more than they'll ever know.

The Arnell family—my in-laws are an incredible group of people who live, laugh, and work hard. They are a tremendous example of what it means to be a disciple of Christ.

The Becoming Your Best team—Jamie, Thomas, Coleman, Heather, and Lara. You are what helps us be successful! Thank you for your tremendous efforts and insights.

The Covenant Communications team—each person is great to work with. In particular, Sam and Kathy have been invaluable with their feedback and many ideas!

Others who have contributed time, energy, or ideas to help make this book a reality include Gary and Jewel Marlowe, Anthony Sweat, Brad Foster, Chris Packard, Brent Weske, Dallin Larsen, Matt Lohmeier, Jeff Flamm, Kirk Chugg, Jen Tanner, Dave Clark, Gaylen Bywater, and Matt Alley.

INTRODUCTION

THOUSANDS OF MISSIONARIES RETURN FROM full-time service every month. You poured your heart and soul into the work. There was little worry about what happened in the world because you were totally focused on sharing the gospel. Then you returned home and were thrust back into a busy and hectic life. It was one of the toughest transitions you will ever make.

Many returned missionaries get lost during that critical period and forget the positive habits they developed on their missions. The statistics for how many returned missionaries go inactive or leave the Church are jaw-dropping. I personally know many returned missionaries who have lost their testimonies or become less active for countless reasons. This trend needs to stop; the Lord needs people He can count on to make a difference in the world—especially after a mission.

This book was written to help returned missionaries successfully bridge that gap between mission life and regular life. The tips, thoughts, and ideas in it will help you build on your mission experience and find true success in life, both spiritually and temporally, as well as help you continue to develop your relationship with Christ and deepen your spiritual conversion. These ideas will help you be a true disciple of the Lord and continue to prepare for His return.

In addition, there are a number of specific "how to" ideas that will help you be successful in whatever you decide to pursue. You will also develop a clear, inspiring vision and set action-oriented goals to make that vision a reality.

Your transition is an incredible opportunity for growth. You'll choose a profession and whom you want to marry. The decisions you make now will impact the rest of your life and generations to come. I hope what you find in this book will provide you with new, powerful insights and ideas to help you truly *return and succeed!*

CHAPTER 1
The Transition

"Brethren, shall we not go on in so great a cause? Go forward and not backward. Courage, brethren; and on, on to the victory! Let your hearts rejoice, and be exceedingly glad."
(D&C 128:22)

YOU'VE JUST COME FROM A structured and disciplined environment. How do you come home and still maintain what you have learned while getting back into the world?

This book will help returned missionaries continue on their upward trajectory and continue to grow and accomplish their dreams. There are too many returned missionaries who have lost their testimonies or fallen away. You may be tempted to put this book down and say, "But it won't happen to me." If we consider past history, we can quickly see that it can and has happened to people who probably used those same words. The fact that you've already read this far is a testament to your desire and willingness to improve.

It doesn't matter whether you served as an elder, sister, an assistant, zone leader, or trainer; what's discussed in this book applies equally. In addition, it doesn't matter whether you served a full mission, had a medical release, or returned early for some other reason. Whatever the case, you can be successful and find joy in your future!

Your mission service is the beginning. It is like a springboard. Now you have "life" ahead of you and the real test of your character and testimony begins. After your mission, nobody will be there to determine how much time you have served each week, how much time you have invested studying the scriptures each day, and how many people you have contacted. Think about all the life-changing lessons you learned during your mission. The individual application of those lessons will be needed as you draw nearer and nearer to the Lord in the coming years.

The first three years after your mission are critical checkpoints that will affect the rest of your life. You will face all kinds of pressures, trials, and demands that will try to pull you away from the Lord and keep you from reaching your full potential. It will take an earnest and sincere effort on your part to "be in the world, but not of the world." Below are two quick examples to illustrate how the pressures of a busy world will try to pull you away from the positive habits you developed on your mission.

Example #1: You're enrolled at a university and have twelve credits. You have classes from 7:30 a.m. to 3:00 p.m. After school, you work from 4:00 to 8:30 p.m. You know when you get home, you have a two-hour project waiting for you and a test the next day.

Example #2: You're working a full-time job from 8:00 a.m. to 4:30 p.m. You have a date from 5:30 to 7:30 p.m. Your home teachers are coming to visit at 8:00 p.m. After the home teachers leave, you lie down on your pillow, exhausted. You look at the clock and it is 9:00 p.m.

In these two examples, where do scriptures, prayer, temple worship, and other key elements of the gospel fit in? As you get into the daily grind of normal life, there will be many *good* things trying to strip you of the *great* habits you developed during your mission. One of your primary opportunities and challenges is to fit back into the world without forgetting what you've learned.

As a returned missionary you will face a crossroads: Will you go back to the life you lived before your mission or continue to build on the positive habits from your mission? Which of these paths will lead you to Christ? For example, many returned missionaries start off with good intentions but slowly let those positive habits slip away. As you apply what you read in this book, it will help you build on the positive habits you learned from your mission and enable you to draw closer to the Lord.

It's not just the intentions that count—it's the actions that will lead us to happiness. As Gandhi said, "Actions express priorities." Your faith and thoughts will determine your actions. Our society is brimming with good intentions, but many times people are lacking on the follow-through. In the following chapters, you'll be able to practice powerful habits that transform intentions into reality and ultimately lead to success.

I have sought the Lord's guidance through fasting and prayer regarding what to share that will help you stay true to Him and be successful in whatever you choose to do. I've also interviewed many returned missionaries and mission presidents to get the best advice possible. The hope is that you will apply what you read and that it will be useful to you as you make the transition from your mission to the rest of your life.

The transition from a mission to a successful life is not easy. When you feel tempted to give up or like it may be too hard or you feel alone, I invite you to always remember this statement:

> *It's not whether you fall down; it's whether you get back up and finish your race.*

The Lord's counsel to Joseph while he was in Carthage Jail can apply to each one of us: "The Son of Man hath descended below them all. Art thou greater than he? Therefore, hold on thy way, and the priesthood shall remain with thee; for their bounds are set, they cannot pass. Thy days are known, and thy years shall not be numbered less; therefore, fear not what man can do, for God shall be with you forever and ever" (D&C 122:8–9).

The transition and journey won't be easy, but they will be worth it. I hope you will be able to find the kind of advice and stories in the following chapters that will make a difference in your life. I wish you wonderful success!

IN A NUTSHELL

What were your First 3 years like?

Busy... Work school Calling Dating ~~Karate~~ Karate

1. The first three years after your mission are critical checkpoints that will affect the rest of your life. You will face all kinds of pressures, trials, and demands that will try to pull you away from the Lord and keep you from reaching your full potential.

2. As a returned missionary you will face a crossroads: Will you go back to the life you lived before your mission or will you continue building on the positive habits from your mission?

games

3. Your faith and thoughts will determine your actions. Our society is brimming with good intentions, but many times people are lacking on the follow-through. Those who practice what is shared in this book will turn intentions into action.

4. You were born of greatness, and you're destined for greatness.

5. It's not whether you fall down; it's whether you get back up and finish your race.

6. The transition from your mission back into the world won't be easy, but you can do it! Always remember, "The Son of Man hath descended below them all. Art thou greater than he? Therefore, hold on thy way, and the priesthood shall remain with thee; for their bounds are set, they cannot pass. Thy days are known, and thy years shall not be numbered less; therefore, fear not what man can do, for God shall be with you forever and ever" (D&C 122:8–9).

CHAPTER 2
Strive to Know the Lord

"And this is life eternal, that they might know thee the only true God, and Jesus Christ, whom thou hast sent."
(John 17:3)

IN THIS TUMULTUOUS WORLD, I don't know of any advice that would be more valuable to you than to strive to know the Lord and follow His counsel. The path of discipleship will get ever narrower for you the closer you are to the Lord. This is exciting and sobering at the same time. Imagine the life of Joseph Smith: he went through some incredible trials and tribulations, but he *knew* the Lord. Was it worth it? Absolutely!

There is no greater joy than the Savior's presence in our lives. He is the great counselor. He knows everything about you and can guide you to happiness. He and His angels continue to minister to people across the earth. Wonderful experiences await the faithful. Before we talk about the temple, scriptures, prayer, goals, or anything else in later chapters, we need to discuss them in the correct context. In other words, we need to address the "why" part of the equation. We can discuss the "how to" in later chapters, but we need to discuss why we attend the temple, pray, serve, etc.

His invitation is to *come unto Him*. As you read the following scriptures, they will start to answer the important "why" question.

D&C 93:1 "Verily, thus saith the Lord: It shall come to pass that every soul who forsaketh his sins and cometh unto me, and calleth on my name, and obeyeth my voice, and keepeth my commandments, shall see my face and know that I am."

D&C 88:67–68 "And if your eye be single to my glory, your whole bodies shall be filled with light, and there shall be no darkness in you; and that body which is filled with light comprehendeth all things. Therefore, sanctify yourselves that your minds become single to God, and the days will come that you shall see him; for he will unveil his face unto you, and it shall be in his own time, and in his own way, and according to his own will."

D&C 84:23–24 "Now this Moses plainly taught to the children of Israel in the wilderness, and sought diligently to sanctify his people that they might behold the face of God; But they hardened their hearts and could not endure his presence; therefore, the Lord in his wrath, for his anger was kindled against them, swore that they should not enter into his rest while in the wilderness, which rest is the fulness of his glory."

D&C 93:19–20 "I give unto you these sayings that you may understand and *know how to worship, and know what you worship,* that you may come unto the Father in my name, and in due time receive of his fulness. For if you keep my commandments *you shall receive of his fulness,* and be glorified in me as I am in the Father; therefore, I say unto you, you shall receive grace for grace" (emphasis added).

ETHER 12:39, 41 (quoting Moroni) "Then shall ye know that *I have seen Jesus,* and that he hath talked with me face to face, and that he told me in plain humility, even as a man telleth another in mine own language, concerning these things; And now, *I would commend you to seek this*

Jesus of whom the prophets and apostles have written" (emphasis added).

"There are goals to gain, summits to climb, revelations to receive. In the eternal scope of things we have scarcely started out on the course to glory and exaltation. The Lord wants his saints to receive line upon line, precept upon precept, truth upon truth, revelation upon revelation, until we know all things and have become like him. Let us press forward in making our callings and elections sure, until, as Joseph Smith said, *we shall have the personage of Jesus Christ to attend us, or to appear to us from time to time*, and until even he will manifest the Father unto us" (emphasis added).[1]

These verses and quotes should fill you with excitement and hope. We have been commanded by the Savior, in His words, to seek Him out. His ministry to the people of the earth continues regardless of Church calling, race, or gender. Hope and wonderful blessings await those who faithfully and diligently serve and seek Him. Always remember, He spent His time ministering to the poor, the sick, and those who recognized their sins. No matter where you have been or what you have done in the past, He can minister to you.

Be cautious of anyone who might teach you this is not possible or that it is only for a select few based on a calling. Christ cautioned "us" in 3 Nephi 29:5–6, "Wo unto him who spurneth at the doings of the Lord; yea, wo unto him that shall deny the Christ and his works! Yea, wo unto him that shall deny the revelations of the Lord, and that shall say the Lord no longer worketh by revelation, or by prophecy, or by gifts, or by tongues, or by healings, or by the power of the Holy Ghost!"

I've met many people inside the Church who believe angels or the Lord will visit only a General Authority. The preceding verse is a clear warning to anyone inside or outside the Church who teaches that the Lord and His angels have ceased ministering to the people of the earth or that this is not possible for you. If you continue faithful, regardless of your calling, the heavens can be open to you in the most literal sense!

A close friend of mine had a remarkable experience while serving as a missionary. Though this story is personal and sacred, he has given me permission to share it here. I share this not to sensationalize the gospel but to illustrate that the heavens are open and the Lord offers us so much more than we realize. The following is from his journal:

> As a missionary, we were asked to give a blessing to the grandmother of a family we were teaching. The daughters happened to be members, but the parents had not been baptized. However, the mother believed what was being taught and they asked us to visit the grandmother in the hospital and give her a blessing—they said she didn't have a long time left. We looked at our calendar and the soonest we could get to her was two days away, plus we had to get permission to leave our area and drive across the city. We obtained the necessary permission and arranged to visit the hospital.
>
> As a side note, I had only been in the mission for three months and devoted every waking moment to memorizing scriptures, the discussions, etc. I was so determined that I was waking up at 4:30 a.m. to study, learn, and memorize. I share that side note because I think that's relevant to why I had the experience.
>
> As we entered the hospital I immediately felt something strong settle over me and knew something was different. As we entered her room I felt something I had never felt up to that point

in my life. Although there were four missionaries in the room, I knew that I was the one who needed to give the blessing. I asked the other missionaries if that was all right and they all felt fine with that request.

Before we even laid our hands on this aged lady, I felt this overpowering feeling; this type of feeling was totally new to me because of its power and strength. As I laid my hands on her head, the strongest spiritual experience I have ever had before or since opened to me. As I try and describe this, it is like trying to describe the taste of salt. I started to bless this lady but simply described what I was seeing with spiritual eyes. I can only describe it as seeing what I could feel with my spiritual eyes. I felt like Nephi of old when he said, "Whether in the body or not I could not tell." I "sensed," "saw," "felt" this lady standing in between our loving Heavenly Father and Christ. I could feel/see their outlines with her in between them. In the background, there were people dressed in a perfect white walking about. The place I was seeing with spiritual eyes can only be described as a place of immense love and joy, incomparable to anything that might exist on earth. This love was so overpowering and all-encompassing it makes any sensation of love felt on earth seem trivial. As much as I love my children and wife, even their births and my wedding do not approach the love that was felt in that place. I felt as if I were on fire, it was wonderful, amazing, incredible . . . there are no words to describe it. It was a place of perfect whiteness above all that is white. A place of perfect love, above any love we can feel on earth. What existed there was beyond all my comprehension.

This lady receiving the blessing had never been introduced to the Church. In this blessing I uttered promises of her future and that she might accept all of these things in their fullness. In one of the only times in my life, the words simply flowed with no thought or effort, and the promises were marvelous—I described and promised her what was shown to me. We then released her from this life and told her that she would suffer no more. We then concluded the blessing.

After the blessing, I had tears streaming down my face and could not speak for nearly twenty minutes. I felt as if I were on fire, something I had never before experienced—even though I'd had a testimony of the Spirit borne to me countless times before. Interestingly, for the next hour I really had no desire to stay on earth. I would have been perfectly happy to die that moment and cross the veil. As we sat on the bus in a South American country returning to our area, I felt so insignificant and was appalled at the nature of the wickedness around us.

The grandma passed away two hours later, and I bore testimony to that family of her future. It wasn't just a belief; it was knowledge.

Nothing in this world compares to what the Savior offers us. When you set your sights on Him, it changes the entire focus regarding the gospel. There is an increased desire to treat people right, to serve both inside and outside the Church, to be compassionate, to abandon any unclean thing, to eliminate contention, to purify your heart, and to obey His personal commandments and direction for you.

The heavens are open. You can receive personal revelation, the sweet whisperings of the Spirit, dreams, and visions that will guide you to the Lord.

Setting your sights on Him is the first and, in my opinion, the most important thing you can do as a returned missionary. This is the "why" part of the gospel. We do the important things so that we can experience His presence according to His time and His will, whether in this life or in the next. There is nothing in this life that can compare. His presence and love trump everything else and make the riches of this world pale in comparison. A focus on Him will guide all of your actions. The specific ideas in the following chapters are all about serving Him and learning how to walk toward His presence.

In a Nutshell

1. The path of discipleship will get ever narrower the closer you get to the Lord.

2. There is no greater joy than having His presence in our lives. He is the great Counselor. He knows everything about you and can guide you to happiness. He and His angels continue to minister to people across the earth, regardless of calling, race, or gender.

3. D&C 93:1 says, "Verily, thus saith the Lord: It shall come to pass that *every soul* who forsaketh his sins and cometh unto me, and calleth on my name, and obeyeth my voice, and keepeth my commandments, shall see my face and know that I am" (emphasis added).

4. "There are goals to gain, summits to climb, revelations to receive. In the eternal scope of things we have scarcely started out on the course to glory and exaltation. The Lord wants his saints to receive line upon line, precept upon precept, truth upon truth, revelation upon revelation, until we know all things and have become like him. Let us press forward in making our callings and elections sure, until, as Joseph Smith said, we shall have the personage of Jesus Christ to attend us, or to appear to us from time to time, and until even he will manifest the Father unto us."

5. Be cautious of anyone who teaches that the Lord and His angels have ceased ministering to the general people of the earth or that this is not possible for you.

6. The heavens are open. You can receive personal revelation, the sweet whisperings of the Spirit, and dreams and visions that will guide you to the Lord.

7. Setting your sights on Him is the first and, in my opinion, the most important thing you can do as a returned missionary. This is the "why" part of the gospel.

CHAPTER 3
Engage in Mighty Prayer

*"And by day have I waxed bold in mighty prayer before
him; yea, my voice have I sent up on high; and angels came
down and ministered unto me."
(2 Nephi 4:24)*

IMAGINE YOU HAVE TWO SONS or daughters. The first talks to you
frequently and shares what happened to them during the day. They
share their concerns and plans with you. They ask for your advice
and thank you often. They tell you multiple times a day how much
they love and appreciate you. The second rarely acknowledges you.
Never asks for advice. Never thanks you for providing for them.
You really do not know what they like because they seldom talk
with you. On the rare occasion when this son or daughter does talk
with you, they say something like "My day was fine" and then walk
past you, barely acknowledging your existence.

As a father or mother, which one would you feel more com-
fortable helping? Which one might you favor as the parent? Which
son or daughter would be more likely to receive your inheritance
as a parent?

This may not be an apples-to-apples comparison, but you
probably get the idea. Certainly God loves all His children. But, as

our heavenly parent, He will abundantly bless and recognize those who acknowledge Him, know Him, love Him, and thank Him. When we hold Him at arm's length, we effectively deny Him the privilege and opportunity to bless us.

Prayer is one of the most effective and powerful ways to develop a strong relationship with Him. Yet it's also one of the most underutilized and underappreciated tools we have in our lives.

Because prayer is so important, asking introspective questions can help keep you in check. Try asking yourself these questions for a quick self-assessment regarding your prayers:

> How much time did you spend praying in the past week?

> Specifically, how much time did you spend on your knees in the past week? Five minutes, ten minutes, thirty minutes, one hour? (Not all prayer takes place on our knees, but this is a useful measurement.)

> How many times would you consider your prayers to be a spiritual experience in the past week?

> How many times do you feel like you really connected with your Heavenly Father while praying in the past week?

These questions are introspective in nature and beneficial because they give us a reality check. On your mission, you probably developed a habit of praying throughout the day, to include both morning and night as a minimum. This is a great foundation to build on!

The title of this chapter uses the word *mighty*. Any prayer that is offered in sincerity and humility will be heard by our Heavenly Father. However, to take it up a level and really get heaven's attention, there is something significant and different about "mighty prayer." To illustrate the difference, think about a significant or traumatic experience in your life. Maybe a loved one was in an accident; maybe you had something happen on your mission; maybe it was a time when you were truly seeking the Lord or repenting of something you had done. In those moments or other moments like them, did you feel a connection with heaven? What was the difference in that type of prayer versus the thirty-second ritual before climbing into bed?

I will be the first to admit that it is difficult to engage in *mighty* prayer on a daily basis. There are probably times when you don't feel like praying. There are probably times when you are tired and ready to climb into bed. Maybe you have been angry or done something you knew was not right—in those cases, sometimes saying a prayer is the last thing you want to do. Those are often the times when we need prayer the most.

When you get home from your mission, not only is it important to build on the habits of daily prayer that you've already established, but it is also important to develop the ability to connect with heaven through mighty prayer and open the windows of revelation to guide you through life.

Look at what the Lord has to say about prayer, and even more specifically, *mighty* prayer:

> 2 NEPHI 4:24 "And by day have I waxed bold in *mighty prayer* before him; yea, my voice have I sent up on high; and angels came down and ministered unto me" (emphasis added).

Is it possible to have angels minister to you? Yes.

> ENOS 1:4 "And my soul hungered; and I kneeled down before my Maker, and I cried unto him in *mighty prayer* and supplication for mine own soul; and all the day long did I cry unto him; yea, and when the night came I did still raise my voice high that it reached the heavens" (emphasis added).

Notice the effort and sincerity with which Enos sought the Lord. He *cried* in *mighty prayer* and didn't cease until he knew his voice had reached the heavens. Notice the pattern of Enos's prayer throughout this chapter. This is a worthy pattern to receive additional revelation.

ALMA 8:10 "Nevertheless Alma labored much in the spirit, *wrestling with God in mighty prayer,* that he would pour out his Spirit upon the people who were in the city; that he would also grant that he might baptize them unto repentance" (emphasis added).

In answer to one person's prayer, the Lord granted Alma's request and rewarded his efforts as he labored among the Nephites.

ALMA 26:22 "Yea, he that repenteth and exerciseth faith, and bringeth forth good works, and *prayeth continually without ceasing*—unto such it is given to know the mysteries of God; yea, unto such it shall be given to reveal things which never have been revealed; yea, and it shall be given unto such to bring thousands of souls to repentance, even as it has been given unto us to bring these our brethren to repentance" (emphasis added).

Could this promise be extended to you as well? Yes!

2 NEPHI 32:8 "And now, my beloved brethren, I perceive that ye ponder still in your hearts; and it grieveth me that I must speak concerning this thing. For if ye would hearken unto the Spirit which teacheth a man to pray, ye would know that ye *must pray*; for the evil spirit teacheth not a man to pray, but teacheth him that he must not pray" (emphasis added).

In those times when we do not feel like praying, we can have a clear knowledge of where those thoughts and feelings originate. It is during those dark moments that prayer may be most needed.

D&C 98:2 "Waiting patiently on the Lord, for your prayers have entered into the ears of the Lord of Sabaoth, and are recorded with this seal and testament—the Lord hath sworn and decreed that they shall be granted."

When you petition your Heavenly Father in sincerity and humility, He will answer your prayers. As you know, it may not be in the time or way you expect, but He *will* answer.

We've barely scratched the surface in these few verses. Notice that one of the common themes from Nephi, Enos, Alma, Moses, and so many others is that after obtaining a declaration about their own status before the Lord, they begin to pray for others.

When you read words in these scriptural verses such as *wrestle* or *cried*, what image comes to your mind? To me, this is so much more than just kneeling for a one-minute canned recitation before climbing into bed. This brings to mind sweat, effort, focus, concentration, and a real desire for answers to questions.

Through the years, I've heard and tried various techniques and approaches that have produced significant fruit. These ideas may help make your prayers mighty and sincere:

- **Go into nature.** Joseph, Nephi, Moses, Mahonri Moriancumer (the brother of Jared), Joseph Smith, and many others went to a mountain or woods to pray. We read in 1 Nephi 18:3, "I, Nephi, did go into the mount oft, and I did pray oft unto the Lord; wherefore the Lord showed unto me great things." If it worked for Nephi, it can work for you.

    When I was at lunch with a good friend, he asked me the question, "Where is your sacred grove?" Great question! I would ask you the same question: where is your sacred grove?

    During the warmer months, I'll often go into the mountains to pray and ponder. One of my favorite things to do is four-wheel on a mountain near our home. I can leave our house and be on a ridge overlooking our valley within thirty minutes. These are almost always special and peaceful experiences.

    One of those experiences came on an early summer morning. I left my house at 5:00 a.m. and went to my "sacred grove" overlooking the valley. It was a brisk morning with a few puffy clouds hovering distantly on the horizon. The first shades of light were just starting to illuminate the horizon as I looked to the east, watching the Uinta Mountains come into view. It took almost thirty minutes until the sun finally crested the horizon. The moment the sun began to appear, I felt its warmth on my face and skin, the remaining darkness was instantly dispelled, and the resulting brightness was too powerful to even look at. It was a beautiful and inspiring moment for me as I stood in awe of the Lord's creations. I knelt down on the ground and thanked our Heavenly Father for the opportunity to witness such a beautiful sunrise and also for the feelings that He impressed upon my soul that morning.

Regardless of your geographical location, nature can provide an incredible setting in which you can commune with the Lord. When possible, go there often. When you are in the mountains or woods or any natural setting, allow the Lord to teach you; don't rush Him. Be patient and listen. There is a reason certain aspects of nature have been likened to a temple.

- **Wait until you feel a "connection."** I remember a lesson shared many years ago in a Church meeting. The teacher decided to change the way he prayed. He indicated that his prayers had become routine and monotonous. He decided to do something different, so he began to address Heavenly Father and then wait until he felt something before saying anything further. I was so impressed with the idea that I tried it the same day he shared his lesson. Sure enough, I addressed Heavenly Father and then waited for almost five minutes until I began to feel a warmth in my chest. The warmth spread throughout my body, and the words that I was to pray flowed clearly into my mind. It was not a routine prayer; this was an inspired prayer from heaven.

  I invite you to try this: address Heavenly Father and then wait until you feel something. Imagine establishing a literal connection, like a light being extended directly to you from Heavenly Father. Once you feel this connection, pray as you feel inspired. As a reminder, you may have to wait longer than you expect to establish that connection. Be patient, and He will respond.

- **Write the thoughts and feelings that come to your mind.** I've found that the more I act on promptings, the more those promptings will come. Conversely, when I do not act on promptings, the number of promptings quickly diminishes. The Lord will trust those who act on His direction.

How many times have you had a good idea and thought to yourself, "This is a really good thought; I need to remember this!"? Then you don't write it down. What usually happens to that idea? Right, it usually disappears. Try writing down a thought or prompting immediately after your prayer, then act on it. I am positive that you will begin to see an increase in personal revelation as you write down your thoughts and then act on them.

- **Ask the question "Is there more, Lord?"** Elder Scott gave a wonderful talk in the October 2009 general conference titled "To Acquire Spiritual Guidance." In it, he discussed the pattern for communing with heaven. After receiving specific, personal guidance, Elder Scott said, "Subsequently I prayed, reviewing with the Lord what I thought I had been taught by the Spirit. When a feeling of peace came, I thanked Him for the guidance given. I was then impressed to ask, "'Was there yet more to be given?'" After asking that question, a flood of new revelation came to him.

How many times are we content with a simple answer when so much more is available? After I read this talk, I went into our kitchen on a quiet evening after our children were asleep and knelt down. I asked the Lord specific questions about my role as a father, as well as some questions about my children. During the prayer, I received clear guidance; it was a beautiful experience. However, after the prayer was over, I didn't stop there; I knelt down again and asked the question, "Lord, is there more?" Indeed, there was more and it was wonderful. I repeated that process three separate times in the same prayer.

I invite you to follow Elder Scott's counsel and ask the Lord, "Is there more?" This simple question is powerful and will reach the heavens if you are willing to hear the answer.

- **Ask the question "What can I do, or whom can I serve today?"**
  This question invites answers. When you ask this question sincerely and are willing to act on the answer, revelation will come. The key is being willing to act on the answer. If we are not willing to act, the answer probably will not come.

When you ask this question, take a moment to pause and quietly wait. Sometimes it takes a few minutes, depending on your sensitivity to the Spirit.

This idea was driven home to me years ago on a rainy evening in South Carolina. It was about eight o'clock on a dark, cloudy evening. One of the people on my home-teaching list was a less-active returned missionary in his midtwenties whom I'll call Jim. He was an airman in the air force, and the only thing I had was a name and a building number where he supposedly lived on base. I felt the prompting to go find this airman, so I put on my jacket and jumped in the car to make the twenty-minute drive to the air force base.

I pulled up to a large four-story building with at least a hundred dorm rooms, and I had no idea where to begin. I looked at the small piece of paper with his name on it to verify the building was correct, and then I bowed my head to say a prayer asking for the Spirit to help me find this returned missionary. These are always opportunities I enjoy because I've seen His hand guide me many times before and I knew He could do it in this case.

I started on the fourth floor, walking past each door, not sure what I was even looking for. I walked all the way around the fourth floor and repeated the same process on the remaining three levels. Nothing!

Feeling slightly dejected, I started walking back to my car, when I felt a distinct prompting to turn around and go back. After whispering another prayer, I returned and repeated the same process.

This time, after going through the top three floors, I walked past a dorm on the first floor, and there in the window was a Book of Mormon. I almost laughed because of how cool it was to see that book sitting there.

I knocked on the door, and a young man with blond hair answered. I asked him if he was Jim, and he responded, "No, but I work with him every day. He sits right next to me at work." It turned out that the less-active returned missionary I was assigned to visit had moved off base and there was no record of where he was. This connection on that dark night was the only way we would have ever found Jim. The person who answered the door that night was also a returned missionary and was impressed when I shared the story of how I came to his door.

Once my new friend gave me Jim's contact information, I called him to set up a visit. Fast forward several months. Jim and I became great friends. He chose to return to full activity in the Church, and the fire was rekindled in him.

This experience wouldn't have happened without a sincere prayer asking for guidance from the Spirit. The Lord loves each of us, and you can be someone's angel in their time of need.

You probably had experiences with this in your mission. With practice and sincerity, rewarding experiences await you if you will ask the question "What can I do or whom can I serve today?" If you're ready to respond to the answer, you can continue to be a significant instrument in the hands of the Lord as He brings about His purposes through you.

- **Pray vocally as well as in your heart.** If we study the scriptures, we will find that we have been commanded to pray in public and in secret. We have been commanded to pray out loud as well as carry a prayer in our heart. I invite you to periodically try praying out loud. Try praying vocally when you are alone and can focus on the words and feelings without worrying about others hearing you.

- **Periodically give a prayer of thanksgiving.** I imagine you have probably done this before. How did it feel to simply express gratitude for all of your blessings without asking for anything? When was the last time you tried this? These types of prayers can be some of the most powerful as we simply express our gratitude to a loving Heavenly Father. If you haven't tried this recently, I invite you to try it today, maybe even right now. Don't ask for anything; simply express gratitude. You may find yourself overwhelmed with a feeling of love.

Trying new ways and places to pray keeps you in tune with the Spirit. The power and effectiveness of your prayers will increase, or, in other words, you will learn to engage in mighty prayer. You are an instrument in the hands of the Lord. Prayer is one of the most important, powerful channels in discovering His will for you. Build on the positive prayer habits you developed during your mission so you can enjoy an increase of revelation in your life and connect with heaven!

IN A NUTSHELL

1. Prayer is one of the most effective and powerful ways of developing a strong relationship with our Heavenly Father. Yet it's also one of the most underutilized and underappreciated tools we have in our lives. *Mighty prayer* can help you connect with heaven. Enos 1:4: "And my soul hungered; and I kneeled down before my Maker, and I *cried* unto him in *mighty prayer* and supplication" (emphasis added).

2. **Go into nature.** Joseph, Nephi, Moses, Mahonri Moriancumer, Joseph Smith, and many others retired to nature to pray. We read in 1 Nephi 18:3, "I, Nephi, did go into the mount oft, and I did pray oft unto the Lord; wherefore the Lord showed unto me great things."

3. **Kneel and wait until you feel a "connection."** Address Heavenly Father and then wait until you feel something. Imagine establishing a literal connection, like a light being extended directly from Heavenly Father to you.

4. **Write the thoughts and feelings that come to your mind.** When you act on a prompting, that's when more promptings and direction will typically come.

5. **Ask the question "What can I do, or whom can I serve today?"** This question invites answers. When you ask this question sincerely and are willing to act on the answer, revelation will come.

6. **Ask the question "Is there more, Lord?"** How many times are we content with a simple answer when so much more is available? Continuing to ask this question invites revelation.

7. **Give a prayer of thanksgiving.** These can be some of the most powerful prayers as we simply express our gratitude to a loving Heavenly Father without asking for anything.

CHAPTER 4
Worship in the Temple Often

*"And the blind and the lame came to
him in the temple; and he healed them."*
(Matthew 21:14)

WHEN WE UNDERSTAND THE TRUE purpose of the temple, it will burn like a fire within us!

One of the greatest additions to spiritual strength is worshipping in the temple often. This is one of the key habits that will help you get closer and closer to the Lord. In this context, *often* means to worship in the temple as often as *you* can.

I've met some who attend once a month and are happy with that, even though their schedule would allow them to attend more often. I've met others who recently had a child and once a month was a significant sacrifice. I have met some who attend weekly and others who attend daily. "Often" means as often as *you* can with your schedule, always remembering that the Lord rewards sacrifice. This also means that it is important to make time rather than excuses. I have interviewed many people for temple recommends, and sometimes I will ask how often a person attends the temple. People will sometimes answer that months or even years have passed because they have been "too busy."

I interviewed a friend (and returned missionary) who had not been to the temple in over a year, despite living less than fifteen minutes from one and having a significant leadership role in the ward. The best time to form the good habits is right when you get home from your mission. You set a foundation that you can build on. Determine now how often you will attend and write it down. In other words, make it a written goal—as discussed in chapter 8.

Take a moment to consider these questions:

What does the endowment symbolize and represent?

How does it apply to you?

What symbols are there in the temple—numbers, colors, shapes, movement, time, people, etc.?

How does something symbolic (such as the veil) become the real thing?

These are key questions we should ponder frequently. Some of the answers may affect what happens to us in the coming eons.

As with scripture study, the Lord rewards effort and sacrifice. I imagine that you probably already have a testimony of temple work. Even so, please allow me to share a few teachings regarding temples. Read these carefully and ask yourself how they could apply to you.

D&C 109:22 "And we ask thee, Holy Father, that thy servants may go forth from this house armed with thy power, and that thy name may be upon them, and thy glory be round about them, and thine angels have charge over them."

D&C 109:26 "That no combination of wickedness shall have power to rise up and prevail over thy people upon whom thy name shall be put in this house."

D&C 110:7–8 "For behold, I have accepted this house [Kirtland Temple], and my name shall be here; and *I*

will manifest myself to my people in mercy in this house.
Yea, I will appear unto my servants [has nothing to do
with a calling], and speak unto them with mine own
voice, if my people will keep my commandments, and
do not pollute this holy house" (emphasis added).

This promise is the real thing; it is the promise that the symbols
and the rituals of the endowment can be real for His servants (you)!

Elder Bruce R. McConkie said in his book *The Promised
Messiah*, "The purpose of the endowment in the house of the Lord
is to prepare and sanctify his saints so they will be able to see his
face, here and now, as well as to bear the glory of his presence in
the eternal worlds."[2]

God has extended great promises if we will worship Him in
His house. It is so much more than just "going to the temple." It is
the sacrifice, the study of the endowment, and the sincere worship
inside the temple that open our hearts and minds to the Lord.

I heard a wonderful story while I was serving in the air force
and living in Tampa Bay, Florida. As this wonderful lady shared
her story during a meeting, I took out my pen and tried to capture
what she was saying to the best of my ability. This is her story as I
recorded it, with names changed for privacy:

> Sister Jones did an endowment in the Orlando
> Temple. She had just finished and was getting
> ready to go home when she felt prompted to
> stay and do one more name. She hesitated be-
> cause the babysitter was at home and she had
> given the babysitter a specific time when she
> would return. But she decided to follow the
> prompting to stay and finish the name for one
> more sister.
>
> On the drive home, she noticed emergency re-
> sponse vehicles in the area. She had a sinking feel-
> ing come over her when she realized they were at
> her house. As she frantically ran into the entryway

of her home, the babysitter cried, "I'm so sorry, I only turned away for a second." Sister Jones's child had been carried away in the canal behind the house and was swept under the culvert, and they still had not found the body. Sister Jones started to run outside to help look for her daughter when she felt a distinct impression that she should look in her daughter's room. As she opened the door to her daughter's room, she found her daughter sitting on the bed all wet and dirty. Sister Jones asked her daughter how she had gotten to her room. Her daughter, however, did not remember how she escaped from the river, only that a nice lady had brought her back to the room. Sister Jones questioned her daughter and asked what the helper's name was. To her astonishment, she recognized that it was the name of the person for whom she had been prompted to stay and finish.

Though we will not all have an experience as plainly miraculous as this sister's, miracles do happen when we worship in the temple. There are so many experiences where the veil becomes quite thin because of sincere temple worship. I have experienced numerous personal, sacred experiences while worshiping in the temple. Indeed, the Lord's promise is true for those who will seek His counsel and guidance within the walls of a temple. For those who have been to the temple only a handful of times, it's probably exciting and still somewhat confusing. If you've attended the temple many times and it feels like it has become boring and mundane, then I suggest you reevaluate the purpose of the endowment and begin to study it carefully.

Below are a few suggestions that may be beneficial to you as you seek to worship in the temple:

- **Attend often.** The quality of temple worship is important, but so is the quantity (when you are physically able to attend often). Something that has been beneficial to me is to plan my week on Sunday and then find a day and time to attend the temple that week. Once it is planned, there will be all kinds of reasons not to attend. Obstacles will appear, and the adversary will try to thwart your efforts. You may have heard the story about the Logan Temple; if not, I'll share it here to illustrate how much the adversary hates temple work and how badly he wants to keep you away from the temple.

Logan Temple President Marriner W. Merrill was sitting in his office one morning in the early 1890s when he heard a commotion outside. Stepping to the window, he saw a great congregation of people coming up the temple hill, some on foot, and others on horseback and in carriages. President Merrill's first thought was, "What will we do with so many people? If we fill every room in the temple, it will not begin to hold them all."

The riders tied their horses up at the hitching posts or turned them loose in the temple corrals and walked complacently about the front grounds, without seeming to have much purpose in mind. They were rather an odd-looking group and were dressed quite shabbily.

They made no effort to enter the temple, so President Merrill went out to greet them and see what he could do for the group. He said to their leader, "Who are you, and who are these people who have taken possession of the temple grounds unannounced?"

He answered, "I am Satan, and these are my people." Brother Merrill asked, "What do you want, and why have you come here?" Satan replied, "I don't like what is being done in the Logan Temple and have come to stop it." That was a bit of a shock to President Merrill, and he answered, "No, we will not stop it. This is the work of the Lord and must go on. You know that you or anyone else can not stop the work of the Lord."

"If you refuse to stop it, I will tell you what I propose to do," the adversary said. "I will scatter this congregation of people throughout these valleys, and we will keep people from coming to the temple. We will whisper in their ears and discourage them from attending the temple. This will stop your temple work."

President Merrill then used the power of his priesthood and commanded Satan and his followers to depart from holy ground. He said that within four or five minutes there was not a person, horse, or buggy in sight. They just disappeared into thin air and were gone.

Then for the next several years, we could have closed the Logan Temple, for very little work was accomplished.[3]

The adversary will do all in his power to stop you from going to the temple. However, when you are sincere in your desire and you make time, the Lord will open the door. It is not so much how busy you are, it is more about finding a day and then making a resolute time.

- **Attend when you are well rested.** Think about your experiences in the temple when you were sleepy versus when you were able to focus on the work. What was the difference for you? It is obviously much easier to have a spiritual experience when you can focus on what is being presented rather than struggle to stay awake. Try to be well rested prior to going to the temple.

- **Take off your watch and leave your phone in the car.** This was an idea someone shared with me over two decades ago.

It is nice to go into the temple and remove the element of time and other distractions. When I take my watch off, it is easier to focus on what is happening and stay in the moment. In addition, it is a symbolic way of removing time from the equation, a reminder that all things are present before the Lord.

When you leave your phone in the car, it's less likely to distract you and others. I was in the changing room one evening while someone's alarm on their phone was ringing. Everyone in the changing room could hear the phone going off, which detracted from the spirit of reverence that should be an integral element in the Lord's house.

- **Study from the best books so you can discover new symbolism and apply it to your life.** When you study from the best books, you will discover things in the temple that you have not thought about before, and it can bring many parts of the temple to life. For example, what does the "circle in the square" represent? How about pillars in the celestial room: how many are there and what do they represent? What is all the symbolism in the sealing room? What about in the baptistry? What do colors and numbers represent? How about levels of progression, both horizontal and vertical? What is symbolic that could represent the real thing?

  These books have enriched my own temple experience and may be a good starting place for you:

  ✦ *The Holy Temple* by Boyd K. Packer

  ✦ *The Day Star* (volumes I and II) by Val Brinkerhoff

  ✦ *The Gate of Heaven* by Matthew B. Brown

  ✦ *The Temple: Gaining Knowledge and Power in the House of the Lord* by Ed J. Pinegar

  ✦ *Sacred Walls: Learning From Temple Symbols* by Gerald E. Hansen Jr.

- **Ponder in the celestial room.** Do not walk right through the celestial room and head toward the exit. Sit down and take time to pray and ponder. Ask the Lord important questions concerning your life and pay attention to your thoughts and feelings. Consider spending time in the celestial room to ponder and pray.

Just a couple of months ago I was in Las Vegas on a business trip. While there, I attended the Las Vegas Temple on a beautiful spring evening. As a side note, I love the symbolism of the Las Vegas temple sitting on a hill overlooking "The Strip," or downtown Las Vegas.

After the endowment session, I took the opportunity to sit in the celestial room. I pondered and prayed while looking at a beautiful, large painting of the Savior. While pondering, a clear and distinct thought came to my mind. It was what the Savior told Peter in Luke 22:31: "And the Lord said, Simon, Simon, behold, Satan hath desired to have you, that he may sift you as wheat." The difference between the scripture and the inspiration I received in the temple was that this was directed toward me! The clear direction used my name, *Rob, Rob.* It suddenly became very personal.

My full thought was this: "Rob, you have an important mission left to fill on earth. Be careful, guard yourself, because Satan desires to have thee and sift thee as wheat!"

Though these words can apply to many people, this message at that moment was directed from our Heavenly Father to me alone. This is the difference between revelation and personal revelation. It can be the same words, but it takes on another level of meaning when it is directed personally at you.

The celestial room is the culmination of the endowment. This is your opportunity to invite revelation into your life.

- **Rotate what you do in the temple**. Rotate between sealings, initiatories, endowments, and the baptistry. Remember that each piece is only a part of the puzzle, and if you are always looking at the same piece, it is hard to see the whole picture. When you rotate events in the temple, you start to see things in their proper perspective, as part of one great whole.

- **Take family names**. Something special happens when you seek out your own family names and take them to the temple. I have witnessed the thin nature of the veil and miracles that happen when we start searching for our own ancestors. If you want to have significant spiritual experiences, prayerfully search out your ancestors and take their names to the temple. Please be careful about using the famous excuse, "My aunt (or uncle) has already done all the work in our family." If you have already searched for names, you know that they are out there. It may not be easy, but many people are surprised by what they find. When you prayerfully begin the search for new names, you may find that those on the other side of the veil will begin helping you. Hence, you open the doors to personal and sacred experiences.

- **Be patient.** Sometimes the ceremony can be confusing or something else about the experience can be frustrating. Don't give up! Eventually these challenges will turn into sweet answers and victories. Persistence will win the day. I have a friend who had several questions about the temple and the gospel. For some, these same questions caused them to lose their testimony. In my friend's case, he patiently waited on the Lord and attended the temple often. After twenty years of waiting, searching, and praying, he finally found his answers. Remember, the Lord's time is not our time and He will teach us when we're ready to learn and act.

Hopefully these ideas will bring the temple experience to life and create a renewed fire within you to attend often and worship with real intent and effort, applying the endowment personally.

As recorded in D&C 109:14, Joseph offered up this counsel and plea during the dedication of the Kirtland Temple: "Do thou grant, Holy Father, that all those who shall worship in this house may be taught words of wisdom out of the best books, and that they may seek learning even by study, and also by faith."

Serving in the house of the Lord has the potential to bring you transcendent joy. You will be richly blessed and rewarded if you maintain this habit throughout your life. Your frequent temple worship will become a spiritual foundation, and you will join the age-old legacy of faithful prophets and believers who were transformed by the experiences they had in God's sacred spaces. Wonderful revelatory experiences await you.

IN A NUTSHELL

1. It's not just about "going to the temple"; it's about worshiping in the temple. Asking questions can change the experience and invites revelation. What does the endowment symbolize and represent? What symbols are there in the temple—numbers, colors, shapes, movement, time, etc.? How does something symbolic become the real thing?

2. Elder Bruce R. McConkie said in his book, *The Promised Messiah*, "The purpose of the endowment in the house of the Lord is to prepare and sanctify his saints so they will be able to see his face, here and now, as well as to bear the glory of His presence in the eternal worlds."

3. **Attend often.** The quality of temple worship is important, but so is the quantity (when you are physically able to attend often).

4. **Study from the best books to discover new symbolism and apply it to your life.** Understanding the symbols of the temple can make the experience deeply personal.

5. **Ponder in the celestial room.** Sit down and use that time to pray and ponder. Ask the Lord important questions about your life and pay attention to your thoughts and feelings.

6. **Rotate what you do in the temple.** Each piece is only a part of the puzzle, and if a person always looks at the same piece, it is hard to see the whole picture.

7. **The temple experience can arm you with power against the adversary!** D&C 109:22 says, "And we ask thee, Holy Father, that thy servants may go forth from this house armed with thy power, and that thy name may be upon them, and thy glory be round about them, and thine angels have charge over them."

CHAPTER 5
Ponder the Scriptures

*"While we meditated upon these things, the Lord
touched the eyes of our understandings."*
(D&C 76:19)

How many times have you felt like the heavens were closed to you? Have you ever felt like you made a valiant effort but were not able to get an answer to your prayers? There were times in my life when I felt the same thing. As I looked inside myself, I realized that typically I was the reason the heavens were closed. Oftentimes it had to do with how much time I invested in the scriptures and also the way in which I studied that had a significant impact on my closeness to the Spirit.

President Henry B. Eyring wisely said, "Reading, studying, and pondering are not the same. We read words and we may get ideas. We study and we may discover patterns and connections in scripture. But when we ponder, we invite revelation by the Spirit. Pondering, to me, is the thinking and the praying I do after reading and studying in the scriptures carefully."[4]

Reading and studying are important, but it is pondering that opens the heavens and invites revelation. Because the world is so busy, it is fairly easy to let this habit of studying and pondering slip away. Technology seems to discourage rather than encourage pondering. The culture in the Western Hemisphere is driven by speed. Certainly we can all do better when it comes to slowing down our busy lives.

Consider these questions:

In the last week, how much time have you actually invested in reading the scriptures?

How much time have you pondered the scriptures in the last week? Ten minutes, thirty minutes, three hours, ten hours, twenty hours?

Do you feel like you were taught by the Spirit when you studied or pondered the scriptures this week? If so, when and how?

It is often helpful to examine what you are actually doing, rather than living a life filled with good intentions and little action. Introspective questions like the ones above provide a quick filter to separate good intentions from reality. Others have benefited from asking themselves these questions often because it helped keep them on track.

Regarding the Book of Mormon, President Ezra Taft Benson said: "Young men, the Book of Mormon will change your life. It will fortify you against the evils of our day. . . . A young man who knows and loves the Book of Mormon, who has read it several times, who has an abiding testimony of its truthfulness, and who applies its teachings will be able to stand against the wiles of the devil and will be a mighty tool in the hands of the Lord."[5] That promise from President Benson is true. When you and I immerse ourselves in the scriptures and make the time to ponder and receive personal revelation, the gospel will come alive and infuse a fire in our souls!

Think about this: have you ever seen a musician perform who *feels* the music? My oldest son is fourteen years old and plays the piano extremely well, but he doesn't just play the music, he *feels* the music. Many people can read the notes and play the music, but the musicians that can *feel* the music are the ones who can bring a musical piece to life. It is the same with the Book of Mormon and the gospel. Many people can read and study the words, but it is the act of *pondering* that will bring them to life. When you ponder the scriptures, you will begin to *feel the music* and the gospel will come to life like a fire burning in your soul. However, if we don't learn to *feel the music*, then we are like the musicians who read the notes but never feel the magic of the music they are playing.

So, how do you really tap into the power of the Book of Mormon (and other scriptures) to *feel the music*? As President Eyring taught, when you ponder the scriptures, it is an incredibly powerful channel to open the heavens through personal revelation. In the end, the personal revelation that comes from a careful study of the scriptures will be a significant contributor toward saving you and me.

As you examine the scriptures below, look carefully at the specific actions that invited the revelation:

> 1 NEPHI 11:1 "For it came to pass after I had desired to know the things that my father had seen, and believing that the Lord was able to make them known unto me, *as I sat pondering* in mine heart I was caught away in the Spirit of the Lord, yea, into an exceedingly high mountain, which I never had before seen, and upon which I never had before set my foot" (emphasis added).

Pondering led to a life-changing revelation for Nephi.

> D&C 138:1 "On the third of October, in the year nineteen hundred and eighteen, *I sat in my room pondering over the scriptures*" (emphasis added).

This led to the wonderful vision by Joseph F. Smith, which is recorded in section 138.

> D&C 88:62 "Verily I say unto you, my friends, I leave these sayings with you to *ponder* in your hearts" (emphasis added).

3 NEPHI 17:3 "Therefore, go ye unto your homes, and *ponder* upon the things which I have said, and ask of the Father, in my name, that ye may understand, and *prepare your minds* for the morrow, and I come unto you again" (emphasis added).

This was the Savior's counsel after He ministered to the people in the Americas.

D&C 43:34 "Hearken ye to these words. Behold, I am Jesus Christ, the Savior of the world. Treasure these things up in your hearts, and *let the solemnities of eternity rest upon your minds*" (emphasis added).

These verses invite us to ponder and treasure up the words of eternal life. When you make an effort to study and *ponder*, you invite revelation and establish the foundation to open the windows of heaven.

In this effort to study and ponder frequently, there are three suggestions that may help:

- **Make time to study and ponder**. Set a time when you won't be interrupted. Set that time aside to study and ponder. The Lord rewards effort and sacrifice.

  Sometimes people feel like their day is maxed out from morning to evening. In that case, consider waking up earlier and using that time to study and ponder. Many people find the evening to be a difficult time to study because they are tired and it is hard to focus. The point is to find a time that works for you and try to stick with it.

  In the last chapter of this book, I'll discuss the power that comes from a strong morning routine. One of the reasons a mission changes lives is because of what missionaries learn to do with their time in the morning and how they start their day. Unfortunately, that morning routine is lost to many returned missionaries.

Let's go back to the introspective questions I asked earlier in the chapter. If you were not happy with your answers, then I have a specific invitation for you.

Are you ready? Some readers may not like this invitation, and others will enthusiastically embrace it. *I invite you to wake up thirty minutes earlier than your current wake-up time and then use that time to read, study, and ponder the scriptures.* If you are getting up at 6:00 a.m., you would get up at 5:30 a.m. While you read, pause to pray and ponder about what you are reading, what it means to you, how it might apply to us as a people or other groups, and so on.

If you do this for a week, I can almost guarantee a spiritual awakening. When you put yourself in an environment to receive revelation, the Lord will usually begin communicating with you. There has never been a single person who said, "Yeah, that didn't really work for me." However, what I hear all the time from people who try this is, "That totally changed my week. I felt more refreshed, I was happier, I was a different person, and I got so much more done than I usually do!" Try this for one week and see what impact it has on your life. The key is to set a time and stick to it. For some this may be easy, and for others it might be very difficult. No matter what your situation, I have confidence in you. You can do it!

Earlier I shared a quote from Gandhi: "Actions express priorities." Good intentions are not enough to open a conduit of revelation; it is our actions that make the difference. Effort and work are the pathway, and they have their reward.

- **When studying, it is not about quantity, it is about quality.** Think about some of the special experiences you've had while studying the scriptures. In many cases, those experiences likely came when you were studying a small handful of verses (maybe even a single verse) and then cross-referencing with other scriptures. It is the pondering of a few verses that often results in spiritual experiences. Think about Joseph Smith when he pondered James 1:5, which led to the First Vision, or Joseph F. Smith as he pondered the third and fourth chapters of Peter from the New Testament prior to the revelation in D&C 138.

A fun idea to try is when you set aside thirty minutes to study and ponder, limit yourself to a total of five verses. From those five verses, ponder their meaning and how they apply to you and your mission in life. If you try this, you might find it to be a rich and powerful experience.

This idea is to simply remind each of us that it is not necessarily how much we read, it is what we do with what we read that matters. For Joseph Smith, that one verse in James 1:5 led him to ponder its meaning at length and resulted in a glorious vision. Maybe there is a verse or a handful of verses that contain a precious piece of doctrine that can unlock a mystery for you. Through careful study and pondering upon what you read, the Lord will open your eyes and reveal his mysteries to you.

Although there have been times when I've read many chapters at once, some of my most sacred experiences came as a result of pondering on just one verse or a small handful of verses. That is why it is often about quality, not quantity.

- **Choose a topic, focus on the topic, and prepare a lesson on that topic.** You probably tried many different forms of reading and studying on your mission. There are so many good approaches. One of the approaches that I found to be effective is to choose a gospel topic and then prayerfully focus on and study that topic. For example, if you were to study the final week of the Savior's life, then that would be a focused topic and would likely take a minimum of several days. Maybe you could study faith, temples, the Second Coming, Gethsemane, the endowment, the Creation, humility, calling and election, the Holy Spirit of Promise, etc.

I remember listening to a talk given by Elder McConkie. I'll paraphrase what he said. He commented that he chose a topic, prayerfully prepared a lesson as if he was going to teach it, and then during the quiet moments on his daily walks he would practice giving the lesson to himself. He said that some of the best talks or lessons were during those quiet moments when he was walking. Many of those talks or lessons he never delivered publicly.

There is a great lesson to be learned from Elder McConkie. Think about this: when do you learn the most—as the teacher or as the student? Certainly we would all answer that we learn more as the teacher. If that is the case, then give this a try. Prayerfully choose a topic and then plan a lesson or talk for that topic. As you prayerfully plan and ponder your lesson, you will find that the Spirit becomes your teacher.

On my hard drive, I have many lessons typed out that I've neither shared nor given in public. The preparation of these lessons was a rich, uplifting, and wonderfully spiritual experience.

If you would like to try this, I invite you to get a piece of paper and prayerfully consider ten topics that you would like to study and learn more about. Write those down and then prepare one lesson or talk a week. After ten weeks, you will have finished your list and I am positive you will have some great experiences in the process. The whole point of preparing a lesson or a talk is that it causes you to ponder about the topic you are studying, and when you ponder, you invite revelation into your life.

- **Try a new approach.** This is simple. If you've become bored or complacent in your current approach to studying the scriptures, then try something new. For example, you could study the scriptures chronologically side by side (the New Testament and Book of Mormon); you could study the scriptures at the bottom of each hymn; you could read the Book of Mormon and underline every reference to Christ (I did this twice in my mission); you could try reading the chapter descriptions of each chapter and go through the entire Book of Mormon in about one or two hours; and so on. The point is that the scriptures should never be "boring" for us and that there are many ways to bring them alive in our personal lives.

On your mission, you were probably in the habit of studying and pondering frequently. However, after the mission, this habit requires upkeep, and the world will constantly try to distract you. In the path of discipleship, studying and pondering the scriptures is one of the key ingredients to understanding the Lord's will for you.

IN A NUTSHELL

1. President Henry B. Eyring wisely said, "Reading, studying, and pondering are not the same. We read words and we may get ideas. We study and we may discover patterns and connections in scripture. But when we ponder, we invite revelation by the Spirit. Pondering, to me, is the thinking and the praying I do after reading and studying the scriptures carefully."

2. How much time have you pondered the scriptures in the last week? Ten minutes, thirty minutes, three hours, ten hours? Do you feel like you were taught by the Spirit when you studied the scriptures this week? If so, when and how?

3. **Feel the music.** Many people can read the notes and play the music, but the musicians that can *feel* the music are the ones who bring a musical piece to life. Many people read and study the words, but it is the act of *pondering* that will bring them to life and help you feel the music!

4. **Make time to study and ponder**. Find a time when you won't be interrupted. Set that time aside to study and ponder each day. The Lord rewards effort and sacrifice.

5. **It's not about quantity, it's about quality**. Think about Joseph Smith when he pondered James 1:5, which led to the first vision, or Joseph F. Smith as he pondered the third and fourth chapters of 1 Peter prior to the revelation found in D&C 138.

6. **Choose a topic, focus on the topic, and prepare a lesson on that topic.** Choose a topic such as the Second Coming, Gethsemane, priesthood, or humility and prepare a lesson on that topic. Some of your best "lessons" may be the ones you prepare but never give.

CHAPTER 6
Choose Your Friends Carefully

"Iron sharpens iron, and one person sharpens another."
(Proverbs 27:17, ESV)

YOU MAY HAVE HEARD THE saying, "You become the average of the five people you spend the most time with." In my experience, that saying is fairly accurate. It lends itself to another adage that says, "Birds of a feather flock together." Friends can be a great strength to you after your mission or they can drag you down.

Pause for a moment and dig back into your past. Did you ever do something you regretted because you felt peer pressure from your friends? Do you think you still would have done it had you not felt peer pressure?

Now, let's turn the tables just a little bit. Have you ever been around someone who inspired and lifted you? What did you want to do after being around them?

Some people you knew prior to your mission will go on to do great things. They will be the type of people who inspire and lift you. You will also find that some people you knew are essentially the same at age thirty as they were when they were seventeen. If you were to spend the majority of your time with one of these two groups of people, which group do you think would help you accomplish your dreams?

Someone shared an experience that illustrates this idea:

> I recently went to lunch with a close friend from high school. During lunch he told me how frustrated he was with his life at that moment. He had not picked up the scriptures or attended the temple for over a year. For the most part, he was not praying anymore. He went out for a weekend with another group of friends (mostly returned missionaries) who were off-roading on Sunday, swearing, and some were even using drugs. On the way home from that weekend, he had an epiphany. He said that although he is in his thirties, he now feels no different spiritually than when he was in high school. He really felt like he had hit a spiritual rock bottom. Fortunately, he was determined to make some changes. As soon as he started making those changes, he felt light start coming back into his life.

Your friends exert an enormous amount of power in your life. Think about my friend in the example above. The people he was associating with weren't inspiring him to be a better person. In fact, it was just the opposite; he felt like he was being lulled into their lifestyle because of their influence.

Let me immediately dispel a thought that some may have. I am not implying that you do not serve and lift others who may be in a difficult circumstance. I am not suggesting that you cannot be friends with someone who is in a tough situation (Christ spent His life with exactly those kinds of people). Everyone encounters difficult circumstances at some point in their lives. But your relationship with your closest friends transcends passing circumstances. Friends help to shape your inner life as well as your outward one. Therefore, it is vital that you think carefully and choose wisely when it comes to your closest friends and those with whom you will spend a lot of time. If the saying "You become the average of the five people you spend the most time with" is true, then you'd better choose those five people thoughtfully!

Ask yourself these questions about your current or potential friends:

> Does this person inspire me and make me want to be a better person?

> Would this person help and encourage me to be successful?

> Does this person radiate positive energy and help me feel good about myself and life?

> Would this person try to sabotage my success or would they help me on the road to success?

> Is this person giving and charitable toward others?

These questions are meant to help you develop a healthy innermost circle of friends and peers. As a reminder, not all relationships require this level of scrutiny. These are the questions I ask about those I spend the most time with.

You can look to the scriptures for examples of how friends direct the course of our lives. Consider the case of Amulek. When he talks about his past, he gives us some valuable clues about the importance of his friends. In Alma 10:4, 6, he says, "And behold, I am also a man of no small reputation among all those who know me; yea, and behold, *I have many kindred and friends*, and I have also acquired much riches by the hand of my industry. . . . Nevertheless, I did harden my heart, for I was called many times and I would not hear; therefore I knew concerning these things, yet I would not know; therefore I went on rebelling against God, in the wickedness of my heart" (emphasis added). This is a clue about Amulek's previous life. Do you think his old friends and family helped him recognize the Lord, or do you think they contributed to his attitude of "rebelling against God"?

Now, let's contrast Amulek's previous friends with Alma. We read about Amulek's relationship with Alma in Alma 15:16, 18: "And it came to pass that Alma and Amulek, Amulek having forsaken all his gold, and silver, and his precious things, which were in the land of Ammonihah, for the word of God, he being rejected by those *who were once his friends and also by his father and his kindred;* . . . Now as I said, Alma having seen all these things, therefore he took Amulek and came over to the land of Zarahemla, and took him to his own house, and did administer unto him in his tribulations, and strengthened him in the Lord" (emphasis added). What an amazing verse of instruction! Amulek lost almost everything. He gave up his friends and even some of his family. At some point, this began to weigh heavily on him. During this difficult time in his life, Alma was there for him, and he was a true friend.

People like Alma are the kinds of friends you should be seeking after your mission. Someone who will "take you to their house, administer to you, and strengthen you in the Lord." In other words, surround yourself with people who care about your success and want to help you grow and develop, both temporally and spiritually.

Amulek's old circle of friends is similar to King Noah's circle of friends. Remember when King Noah feared Abinadi and was ready to release him? However, the priests (his friends) convinced him that he was a righteous man and that Abinadi was the wicked one—the power and influence of friends!

Let's look at one more example in 3 Nephi 7:6: "And the regulations of the government were destroyed, because of the secret combination of the friends and kindreds of those who murdered the prophets." If we could really dive into this story and go back in time, how do you think these friends arrived at the point where they were murdering the prophets? Can you imagine these "friends" sitting in a room discussing what they were going to do next and how they were going to do it? These people who murdered the prophets were heavily influenced by their "friends" to do something they may never have considered otherwise.

We see in those examples the power of friends for good or for bad. It is our decision whom we choose to bring into our close circle of friends.

The following ideas can help you to find and develop great friendships:

- **Ask the questions from the early part of this chapter about your current circle of friends.** This might be a tough activity, but it will be revealing and helpful to you in the future.

  What I say next may rub some people the wrong way. If you currently have some close friends and you cannot answer those example questions in a positive way, then consider cutting ties with them. It does not mean you cannot occasionally meet with them or say hi, but do you really want one of your closest friends to drag you down or be a deterrent to your progress?

  This is not easy to do. In fact, it may be tremendously difficult. But we are talking about your life and salvation. Remember Amulek: earlier in his life, his friends were a hindrance to his progress. Later in life, Alma was a great help and support to his progress.

  Although it is difficult to change your circle of close friends, you might find this to be one of the most beneficial things you ever do.

- **Create a mastermind group.** The idea of a mastermind group may be a new concept to some. A mastermind group can help you be successful both spiritually and temporally. It can help you see things you might not otherwise have seen or help you remove a personal roadblock and see something in a new way. Once you've experienced the power of a mastermind group, you'll see how valuable it can be in your life. A mastermind group is a group of people you meet with to bounce ideas off each other, share your challenges, and network together. For example, I recently attended a mastermind group with several friends. I sat at a table with five other people, and we each took about thirty minutes discussing different opportunities and challenges. There was great feedback from the group, and several of them had connections with different people who could help us.

To start a mastermind group, find a small group of three to eight people. Choose a time to meet with this group, perhaps every month or every quarter, and use them as a sounding board: bounce ideas off of them, ask them for advice, share your plans for the future, and get their opinions. The group will do the same for each individual in turn.

To start a mastermind group, you can invite people who already inspire you. You can also post an advertisement on a university board or in a newspaper. It is actually beneficial if the people in your mastermind group are not exactly like you. People of varying strengths and personalities will enrich your group, as long as you get along and they support your success. The most important part of a mastermind group is that you do not invite anyone who is selfish. They should be excited about other people's successes, and they should be contributors during your mastermind meetings. It doesn't really matter where you meet. You can meet in an apartment, a home, or a conference room. Masterminding has changed my life, and this is a habit that can change yours as well.

- **Stay close to those who inspire you.** Make a plan or resolution to stay in close contact with those who inspire you. If you developed a friendship with another missionary, don't let that friendship fade after the mission. Call each other at least once a quarter or go out for lunch periodically, if this is geographically possible. You can also stay in contact through platforms such as Facebook or Twitter, but don't just limit yourself to passively looking at your friend's content. If you live far away from each other, you can video chat one-on-one or with a group. It's a great way to stay connected and much better than just talking on the phone. Social media provides remarkable opportunities to stay connected as long as you use them to foster relationships, not just to keep vague tabs on each other.

In order to maintain a friendship and keep it alive, often-times you will need to be the catalyst, the one who makes the call. Those relationships will continue to bless your life in many different ways.

This simple piece of advice is what led to me finding my wife. After my mission, I stayed in close contact with several missionary buddies, and within about six months of being home, I decided to room with one of my former companions at Utah State. He had a four-person room in a particular apartment complex, which happened to be the same apartments where my future wife was living that year. Had I not stayed in close contact with my mission companion and decided to be his roommate, I probably wouldn't have met my wife. Aren't I grateful for his friendship!

Your friends will play a critical role in your success in life. For some, this will mean a serious transition to change friends. It's not easy to change your circle of friends. If this is something you feel is right and you commit to change, but you're not sure how to do it, talk to someone you really trust such as your bishop, parent, coach, or maybe even an institute instructor. It might be beneficial to get two separate opinions. I had a close friend say to me, "Toxic people will contaminate your life. You need to get the toxicity out of your life!" Sometimes this may even require something as dramatic as moving to a different city. Every situation will be different, which is why I suggest getting some advice from someone you trust and respect.

The relationships you build will help you both temporally and spiritually. Choose wisely and choose carefully those you spend your time with. Your friends will inspire you to great heights if you choose the right friends!

IN A NUTSHELL

1. You may have heard the sayings "You become the average of the five people you spend the most time with" and "Birds of a feather flock together." Friends can be a great strength to you after your mission, or they can drag you down. You get to choose your circle of friends.

2. When thinking about whether to invite someone into your *close* circle of friends, consider asking yourself these questions:

   Does this person inspire me and make me want to be a better person?

   Would this person help and encourage me to be successful?

   Does this person radiate positive energy and help me feel good about myself and life?

   Would this person try to sabotage my success, or would they encourage my success?

   Is this person giving and charitable toward others?

3. **Create a mastermind group.** Find a small group of three to eight people. Choose a time to meet with this group, perhaps every month or every quarter. Use this group as a sounding board: bounce ideas off of them, ask them for advice, share your plans for the future, and get their opinions. Do the same for them in return.

4. **Stay close to those who inspire you.** This can include people you met on your mission. Resolve to stay in close contact with those who inspire you; for example, if you developed a friendship with another missionary, don't let that friendship fade after the mission. Call each other at least once a quarter or go out for lunch periodically. You'll find that you are the one who needs to be the catalyst, so don't wait for others.

CHAPTER 7
Develop a Clear Personal Vision

"For behold, this is my work and my glory—to bring to pass the immortality and eternal life of man."
(Moses 1:39)

I HAVE BEEN FORTUNATE TO travel all over the world to meet with political and business leaders, presenting seminars to large and small organizations, and I have seen firsthand the effect that a clear vision has on a person, family, team, and company.

A vision is something that clearly describes who you are, what you want to become, and what impact you want to leave on the world. A vision is not a list of goals. I will discuss how to set effective goals in the next chapter, but first you have to have a purpose or a vision. The vision is the "why" that drives your goals. Goals should support and help you accomplish your vision.

A vision charts the course for your future. An airplane doesn't take off without a flight plan, and a ship doesn't leave the harbor without a charted course and a rudder.

Some of the greatest concerns returned missionaries share have to do with determining their course: "What am I going to do with myself in the future? Where will I go to college, and what will my major be? What will I do for a career?" This is why you would develop a personal vision, to help answer those questions and give you a clear purpose after your mission.

Recently, my father and I returned from a three-day Leadership and Success Boot Camp in Kigali, Rwanda, for two hundred entrepreneurs. Years ago, in 1994, approximately 1.1 million Rwandans were killed in a horrific genocide over the course of just one hundred days. What makes this massacre even more tragic is that it was neighbor killing neighbor, and in most cases, it was done using a machete. Finally, after one hundred days, the international community intervened to stop the massacre and replaced some of the government officials who were responsible. During our visit, we saw buildings still riddled with bullet holes twenty years later.

With that brief history as a backdrop, we had the opportunity to meet with their president, President Kagame, in their version of the White House. President Kagame was the general who had led the revolution twenty years ago to overthrow the corrupt government. When he took office, he faced an almost impossible task: reuniting a country whose neighbors were responsible for killing each other and whose people were divided into two groups, one being considered superior to the other.

Imagine being in his shoes. What could you possibly do to unite the country? Well, the first thing he did was eliminate the different social classes and labeled everyone a Rwandan. Second, they came up with a method to bypass the judicial system to move past the genocide. They had almost two hundred thousand people responsible for killing others, and there was no way to put that many people through the judicial system. They determined that if the guilty person would confess to the village, share exactly how many people they killed, how they did it, and where they put the bodies, the neighborhood and country would need to forgive them. Amazingly, that worked! Finally, President Kagame developed a clear vision for the country called "Rwanda 2020." The vision is *to be a unified, middle-income country on the global stage by 2020 as Rwandans.* Incredibly, everyone has bought into his vision. The country is unified, and there is hope where there was once despair.

Each member of the country sees a way forward, and they are working together to overcome serious hurdles to achieve that vision. Rwanda now has one of the fastest growing economies in Africa, and there is a palpable sense of hope and excitement in that country.

That is the power of a clear vision!

A personal vision may also be intensely transformative. I spoke some time ago to the students at a local high school. A couple of days later, a mother called and asked if I would coach her son. I asked her what his story was and why she was asking. This is a brief summary of the story she shared with me.

Her fifteen-year-old son, whom I'll call John, was a counselor at a BSA Scout camp. While at the camp, another counselor (one of his closest friends) was killed by lightning in a terrible accident. After the accident, John's father drove to the Scout camp to pick up John and bring him home. John had his learner's permit, so his father decided to let John drive home through the winding mountain roads while they talked. During the drive, John accidentally drifted off the road and rolled their truck down the hill. When the truck was done rolling, John looked over, and to his horror, his dad was dead.

Can you imagine the trauma of losing your best friend and father within a couple of days? In addition, don't you think John felt responsible for the death of his father?

I decided to help coach John and do whatever I could to support him. His mother came to our office with John, and we visited for a while. After discussing a few different success principles, we started talking about his vision for the future. Not surprisingly, he did not have one. He felt lost. He felt hopeless. He felt like he had no future.

We talked about how to develop a vision, and then I gave him about fifteen minutes to come up with his own personal vision. For him, it ended up being about two paragraphs. As he read his newly developed vision, tears streamed down his mother's face. His vision was filled with hope and direction. It was a truly inspiring moment in my life that I will never forget. In that small amount of time, he went from being a person without a rudder to having a clear direction about who he was and what he wanted to become. He still has a long and difficult road ahead of him, but now he can face those challenges and move forward with a purpose.

The Lord himself has revealed his vision for us in Moses 1:39. "This is my work and my glory—to bring to pass the immortality and eternal life of man." That is a very clear vision described in just one sentence!

You can work on developing your own clear vision using some key exercises. Use your computer, pull out a pen and paper, or feel free to write your answers in this book.

Please answer the following questions prior to writing your vision. These questions are designed to get the creative juices flowing and to help you think about who you want to become and what legacy you want to leave. Take about two or three minutes per question.

Where would you like to be in five or ten years from now (married, type of job, things you want to accomplish, etc.)?

Think of a mentor or a person you know who inspires you. What traits, qualities, and characteristics do they possess that you admire?

Fifty years from now, as people look back on your life, how do you hope they will describe you?

Take a couple of minutes to ponder and reflect on your answers.

Now, with the answers to these questions at the forefront of your mind, write your vision. Use the present tense, such as "I am," rather than phrases like "I want to; someday; in the future; I hope." Stating your vision in the present causes you to create the mental reality prior to the physical reality. For example, "I am a person of deep character. I am loyal and faithful to the Lord."

Pause here to write your own personal vision.

How was that experience for you? This is often life-changing for people. In seminars, when I ask how many people have a clearly written personal vision, usually less than 1 percent raise their hand. We have done this simple exercise with leaders around the world, and it has had a huge impact on many of them. Very few people take the time to step back and think about these things. I hope this activity was beneficial to you and that your personal vision will serve as a beacon and guide for you. This is oftentimes akin to adding a rudder to a ship. It gives you a clear sense of who you are and what you want to become in this life. Now when you set goals, you can do so with a clear purpose and an end in mind.

I suggest putting your vision in a place where you will see it often, such as next to your computer or your bed. You can also download a great app called *Life Organizer* to keep your vision and goals in front of you constantly.

As a returned missionary, one of the most important things you can do is develop a clear vision. All you have to do is look at your fellow missionaries about five years after the mission. You will probably be able to identify which ones had a clear vision and which ones did not.

When you have a clear vision that inspires you, it will help guide your decision making. Your vision should cause you to be excited to get up in the morning because of your purpose. When you do set goals, those goals will be there to help you accomplish your vision.

Finally, I invite you to reflect on your vision at least monthly, if not more often. Memorize it. Let it guide your decision making. You were born for greatness, and your future is bright. This is one of the key steps in setting yourself up for success, both temporally and spiritually!

IN A NUTSHELL

1. A vision is something that clearly describes who you are, what you want to become, and what impact you want to leave on the world. A vision is your "why," or your purpose. It is not a list of goals; goals come later and are the means to make your vision a reality.

2. To get your mind thinking about what might be a part of your personal vision, ask these questions:

   Where would you like to be five or ten years from now (married, what type of job, things you want to accomplish, etc.)?

   Think of a mentor or someone you know who inspires you. What traits, qualities, and characteristics do they possess that you admire?

   Fifty years from now, as people look back on your life, how do you hope others will describe you?

3. It's better to write your vision using the words "I am . . ." rather than "someday" or "I hope to . . . ." In other words, create the mental reality prior to the physical reality.

4. Download the *Life Organizer* app to keep your personal vision in front of you.

5. In seminars, we've found that less than 1 percent of people have a personal vision. Your personal vision will serve as a beacon and guide for you. This is oftentimes akin to adding a rudder to a ship. It defines who you are and what you want to become in this life. Now when you set goals, you can do it with a clear purpose and an end in mind.

CHAPTER 8
Set SMART Goals to Accomplish Your Dreams

"It is most appropriate to set some serious personal goals in which you will seek to improve by selecting certain things you will accomplish within a specified period of time. You are the leaven on which the world depends; you must use your powers to stop a drifting and aimless world."[6]

MY FATHER HAS A GREAT saying: "A vision without a plan is like a tiger without teeth." A vision provides the direction and purpose, and goals are how you make the vision a reality.

Begin by asking yourself these questions: What are some things that you would really like to accomplish in the next year? Are any of those things clearly written in the form of a goal?

During the past four years, we've researched the power and effectiveness of goals. We've found that people are around 90 percent more likely to accomplish something if they have a clearly written goal. That is a huge deal . . . 90 percent more likely to accomplish something if it is clearly written in the form of a goal! Yet, on average, only 10 percent of people have clearly written goals.

There are many reasons not to set goals. Perhaps you never learned how. You may feel too much accountability once a goal is written down, or too much guilt if you fail to accomplish it. Perhaps you've tried to set goals about things you didn't truly want to do, so instead you let them slide. All these things can be overcome if a person understands the real purpose of goals and learns how to use them.

I have a friend who is an accountant with several children. He is successful and has a seemingly great life. However, we were talking one day, and he said that he felt empty. He felt like he could accomplish more and do more. I asked him about goals, and he responded, "I have never really set a goal in my life." We talked about effective goal-setting for a few minutes, and he decided to give it a try. That year, he developed five specific goals. One goal was to run a 5K in less than thirty minutes prior to July 30. To his amazement, he accomplished all five of his goals by the end of the year. In his words, he said, "I would not have done a single one of these five things had they not been written in the form of a goal." He is now a believer in the power of goals, and he set a lot more for the next year.

For my accountant friend, goals took the impossible and made it possible. I have seen it have the same effect on people all over the world. Goals can impact every area of your life.

Below are the steps to effective goal-setting. I invite you to pause and try these steps right now in your own life.

- **Review your vision.** Your goals should support your vision. It is important to remind yourself of your vision prior to setting your goals. The vision is the purpose or destination, and the goals are the way to make the vision a reality.

- **Determine your roles.** These would be your specific roles in life. For example, some of your roles might be brother or sister, son or daughter, disciple, employee (whatever your job title is), citizen, friend, your Church calling title, etc. One of your most important roles is "personal." The role of "personal" refers to your physical, mental, spiritual, and emotional well-being.

    Sometimes people set goals, but they really only focus on one or two areas of their life. By dividing your life into your most important roles, it helps keep you balanced and causes you to think about what you can accomplish or do in each area of your life. In my experience, setting goals through roles is helpful in maintaining a balanced approach to life. It helps keep a person focused on their priorities and on what matters most.

- **Set SMART goals under each role**. This is one of the keys to effective goal-setting and the hardest area to get right. I have worked with CEOs and every level of leader who typically struggle with this in the beginning. The more practice they get, the easier it becomes. I have heard people say, "I used to set goals, but now I realize they weren't well written and that's why I didn't get the outcomes I was hoping for." Goals become SMART goals when they are specific, measurable, achievable, relevant, and time specific.

  - **Specific:** The more specific a goal, the more likely it is to be achieved. Tell me which one of these examples you think is better: *Lose weight* or *Be at 135 pounds by October 30*. Of course, the second example is better because it is more specific and easier to develop a plan for. Yet I have seen the first example used many times as a goal. Try to make your goals very specific.

    Furthermore, the second example is positively phrased. Positive goals feel more achievable and are more motivating than negative ones. Notice how I didn't say "lose fifteen pounds"; I put a target weight rather than "lose" the weight.

  - **Measurable:** At the end of the year, you should be able to look back at your goals and objectively say, "Yes, I did" or "No, I didn't" accomplish them. A measurable goal increases accountability and is more likely to help you accomplish it. Here is another example: *Have a great relationship with my wife* versus *Go on at least two dates a month without the children*.

The second example is a better goal because it is measurable. The first example is a nice vision but a poor goal because it is neither specific nor measurable. The first example allows for a lot of wiggle room, but the second example will cause you to be accountable because it is either a "yes" or "no" goal.

- **Achievable:** Your goals should stretch you and maybe take you outside your comfort zone, but they should still be achievable. If you are a sophomore in college, it may not be realistic to set a goal of earning $10 million in the next six months if you have $1,000 in your account. If a goal is unachievable or even just too difficult, a person is more likely to become discouraged and give up.

- **Relevant:** Your goals should be relevant to your vision. If a part of your vision is *I am a healthy and well-rounded person*, then you might want to include goals about health and exercise.

- **Time-Specific:** If possible, add a date or time to your goal. For example, *I will finish a 5K in less than twenty-eight minutes by July 21,* or *I will go on at least two dates a week.* When there is a time or date attached, it increases accountability.

- **Send your goals to 3–5 people.** This step will increase the likelihood of you accomplishing your goals by 33 percent.[7] Once you develop your annual goals, try sending them to three to five people you trust and admire. Make sure you tell them why you are sending them your goals. Report back to them at the end of the year. I have been doing this for almost eighteen years with my family and several close friends. They enjoy getting my goals for the new year as well as my report from the previous year, and I appreciate their feedback. I can

tell you from firsthand experience that when I'm waffling on whether or not to finish a goal halfway through the year, this reporting at the end of the year always comes to mind and usually drives me to finish the goal. This important step will help you stay accountable. Pause right now to think of a few people with whom you could share your goals.

- **Reference your goals often.** Don't go through all the effort of developing your goals and then let them sit in a drawer. Review them at least once a week. Put them in a place where you can see them. As I mentioned earlier, the *Life Organizer* app is a great tool to keep your goals in front of you.

Those are the steps to set effective goals. Anyone can do it and it is a game-changing habit. If you adopt this single habit, you will be in the 10 percent of people who actually set clearly written goals. Many people find a reason to avoid coming up with specific goals. If you've read the book this far, my guess is that you are an action taker, and I am sure you will find a great sense of accomplishment in developing your goals.

Before you develop or refine your goals, let's make sure we have the SMART aspect down. You can be my coach. How would you coach me and change these goals from wishful thinking to achievable SMART goals?

Be a great home teacher.

Attend the temple often.

Be healthy this year and lose weight.

Be kind to others.

Here are some possible answers, though yours will vary:

Visit every home teaching family at least one time a month and send a birthday card for every birthday.

Attend the temple at least twelve times before December 30.

Run a 5K in less than twenty-eight minutes before July 30 OR be at or less than one hundred sixty-five pounds before September 25.

Send a note in the mail to at least two friends every week.

The switch from vague wishes to SMART goals dramatically changes how your goals can motivate you and make it possible for you to achieve great things.

As you develop your goals, do it around the things you can control. For example, it may not be a bad goal to say *win the state championship as a basketball team this year*, but a better personal goal would be something like *after every practice, exercise for an additional twenty minutes and take one hundred free-throw shots.* Although the state championship goal is not bad, there are a lot of variables you cannot control. In the second example, you have total control over your goal.

Now, I invite you to pause and develop your annual goals for the remainder of this year. If you already have goals, I invite you to refine them as necessary or send them to your friends. Before you start this process, please include one powerful step: Pray for Heavenly Father's guidance and direction for you!

It is important to realize that plans and goals will not always go as you expect. Things will happen that will require you to alter your plan. But don't let this discourage you from setting goals anyway. Always remember that it is better to shoot for the stars and hit the moon than to not shoot at all. I had a person once say, "I'm not a goals guy." It is difficult to help someone who has no desire. We may have the tools, but if we don't use them, nobody can help us. If you are reading this book, I assume you have the desire and I applaud you!

Finally, the reason for setting goals is not to check them off a list. The reason to set goals is to enjoy the journey. Make sure you never lose sight of that. The goal will start you on the journey, so make sure you enjoy it!

IN A NUTSHELL

1. A vision without a plan is like a tiger without teeth. A vision provides the direction and purpose, and goals are how you make the vision a reality.

2. A person is 90 percent more likely to accomplish something when they have a clearly written goal. Yet, on average, only 10 percent of people have clearly written goals.

3. Follow these steps to set effective and actionable goals:

   Review your personal vision. The reason to come up with goals is to make this vision a reality.

   Determine your roles. For example: student, brother, sister, Church member, manager, etc. You'll set goals within each role to help you maintain balance.

   Set SMART goals in each role. The way you write a goal will be critical to ensuring that you accomplish it.

   Specific: The more specific a goal, the more likely it is to be achieved.

   Measurable: A goal is best when it's objective. Ask whether you can measure it.

   Achievable: A goal should stretch a person but still be achievable.

   Relevant: It should be relevant to your vision.

   Time-specific: It should have a date or time attached to it.

4. **Share your goals with a group of 3–5 people.** This step increases the likelihood of a goal being accomplished by 33 percent.

5. Pray for Heavenly Father's direction and guidance when developing your goals!

CHAPTER 9
Lead with Love

"Wherefore, my beloved brethren, if ye have not charity, ye are nothing, for charity never faileth. Wherefore, cleave unto charity, which is the greatest of all."
(Moroni 7:46)

THE LORD CAN UTILIZE YOU to accomplish His purposes. He needs leaders who will lead with love, charity, and compassion. He needs leaders who will set an example and teach by the Spirit.

Leadership callings in the Church can be a great blessing, as I'm sure you have experienced at some point in your life. Callings give us the opportunity to learn, meet amazing people, and roll up our sleeves to serve others.

At the same time, callings can drive a wedge between people, create hard feelings, and hurt relationships. In the Church, we are a bunch of imperfect people trying to grow, develop, and serve together. There will be speed bumps along the way.

If you are called to a leadership position, you have a solemn responsibility to be humble, seek the guidance of the Lord, and lead with love. If you don't, you will be accountable to Him.

I invite you to apply the following scriptures only to yourself. These scriptures pertain to both men and women, but I want to highlight a specific warning directed toward holders of the priest-hood. It is not that women can sit back and ignore these warnings, but these particular verses are a voice of warning to those who hold the priesthood:

> D&C 121:39–44 "We have learned by sad experience that it is *the nature and disposition of almost all men*, as soon as they get a little authority, as they suppose, they will *immediately begin to exercise unrighteous dominion.* Hence *many are called, but few are chosen.* No power or influence can or ought to be maintained by virtue of the priesthood, only by persuasion, by long-suffering, by gentleness and meekness, and by love unfeigned; By kindness, and pure knowledge, which shall greatly enlarge the soul without hypocrisy, and without guile— Reproving betimes with sharpness, when moved upon by the Holy Ghost; and then showing forth afterwards an increase of love toward him whom thou hast reproved, lest he esteem thee to be his enemy; That he may know that thy faithfulness is stronger than the cords of death" (emphasis added).

Whether you're an elder or sister, when you apply this standard to yourself, it should probably cause you to feel uncomfortable. I know there are times in my life when I have been guilty of exercising unrighteous dominion or compulsion as a leader or parent. I have tried to repent of that. It is so much easier to simply tell someone what to do and how to do it rather than to lead with love and gentleness. As a former fighter pilot, I confess that it is a constant internal battle for me to patiently lead and love rather than direct and tell.

However, this is the standard the Lord has set for His lead-ers. When a leader exercises unrighteous dominion or compul-sion rather than leads with love, they should repent quickly and earnestly. Remember, it is the disposition of nearly *all men* to lead with unrighteous dominion, and that is not the Lord's plan. That is not the path to exaltation.

As if this isn't hard enough to do in a leadership calling, the Lord also expects us to lead with love in the home. The home is where the true measure of a man or woman will be assessed.

Now, let's go back a few verses in Section 121 and see if we can identify why many are called but few are chosen:

> D&C 121:34–38 "Behold, there are many called, but few are chosen. And why are they not chosen? Because their hearts are set so much upon the things of this world, and aspire to the honors of men, that *they do not learn this one lesson—That the rights of the priesthood are inseparably connected with the powers of heaven*, and that the powers of heaven cannot be controlled nor handled only upon the principles of righteousness. That they may be conferred upon us, it is true; but when we undertake to cover our sins, or to gratify our pride, our vain ambition, or to exercise control or dominion or compulsion upon the souls of the children of men, in any degree of unrighteousness, behold, the heavens withdraw themselves; the Spirit of the Lord is grieved; and when it is withdrawn, Amen to the priesthood or the authority of that man. Behold, ere he is aware, he is left unto himself, to kick against the pricks, to persecute the saints, and to fight against God" (emphasis added).

Understanding this scripture is critical to becoming an effective leader and connecting with heaven. These verses should cause all of us to take a serious look at our own lives and humbly ask ourselves whether we fall into any of those categories.

Is our heart set upon the things of this world?

Do we aspire to the honors of men?

Do we seek to cover our sins?

Do we try to gratify our pride or vain ambitions?

Do we exercise unrighteous dominion in our callings or in our homes?

These may not be "feel good" questions, but if you have been ordained to any office in the priesthood, they are essential to ask if you claim any hold on the priesthood. If we cannot answer them in the way the Lord expects, then "Amen to the priesthood or the authority of that man." Ouch! We'd better be paying attention to these verses.

I won't answer this question, but you have seen the statement twice in two separate verses illustrated above, "Many are called, but few are chosen." Chosen for what? The answer to this question is much more significant than it appears at first glance. When you think about the word *chosen*, carefully think about where you hear this in the temple.

> D&C 95:5–6 "But behold, verily I say unto you, that there are many who have been ordained among you, whom I have called but few of them are chosen. They who are not chosen have sinned a very grievous sin, in that they are walking in darkness at noon-day."

This scripture is addressed to members of the Church, specifically ordained men. For all who lay any claim to the priesthood, understanding this verse is of utmost importance. Look carefully at these words: *many have been ordained, but only a few of them are chosen.* I invite you to study, ponder, and pray about the answer to that question: Chosen for what? The admonition in section 95 is that very few of us who are ordained have been chosen; those are not my words but the Lord's.

Regarding both men and women, the Lord needs more leaders and Saints who are kind, compassionate, and loving. How you and I live and lead will determine whether the Lord chooses us. Many will be ordained, but the question is how can you learn the *one* lesson and develop the ability to lead with love so the Lord can choose you in His time?

When we talk about leading with love, have you considered that a person called to lead may be on trial as much as the people whom they are called to lead? In other words, have you considered that the Lord might be testing the leader as much as the follower (if not more)?

Here is a hypothetical question for you to ponder. How do you think the Pharisees would respond if they were asked whether they were the ones being evaluated and judged? They dressed in their fine clothes and sat in their judgment seats. Although they were the recognized spiritual leaders of their time, they were the ones responsible for crucifying our Lord. I am sure that most of them never even considered they were the ones on trial.

I love reading this inspired statement from President Uchtdorf in his October 2008 general conference address "Lift Where You Stand":

> There is a better way, taught to us by the Savior Himself: "Whosoever will be chief among you, let him be your servant."
>
> When we seek to serve others, we are motivated not by selfishness but by charity. This is the way Jesus Christ lived His life and the way a holder of the priesthood must live his. The Savior did not care for the honors of men. . . . Throughout His life, the Savior must have often felt tired and pressed upon, with scarcely a moment to Himself; yet He always made time for the sick, the sorrowful, and the overlooked.
>
> In spite of this shining example, we too easily and too often get caught up in seeking the honors of men rather than serving the Lord with all our might, mind, and strength. . . .
>
> The Lord judges so very differently from the way we do. He is pleased with the noble servant, not with the self-serving noble.[8]

The excerpt above from President Uchtdorf is inspired. I invite you to consider how you treat others when you are called to serve in a leadership position, including the most important leadership position of being a mother or father. This is a reminder to all of us not to aspire to the honors of men and hope to be the Relief

Society president, bishop, elders quorum president, etc. In fact, be careful about envying those positions because if you are called to those positions of leadership, you will also be accountable to the Lord for what you did and how you led others. It is the leader who is often being tested, so be willing to serve, but be careful what you aspire to. As a leader in any capacity, always beware of gossip, premature judgment, and sometimes even arrogance.

This is the difference between someone who may have authority versus someone who has power in the priesthood. Just the other day I was talking with someone, and I asked them the question, "Is it possible to have authority but no power?" The answer is clearly yes! In fact, if we believe what is taught in both D&C 95 and 121, then there may be more of us than we care to admit in that camp who have authority and no power. Elder Boyd K. Packer said, "We have done very well at distributing the authority of the priesthood. We have priesthood authority planted nearly everywhere. We have quorums of elders and high priests worldwide. But distributing the authority of the priesthood has raced, I think, ahead of distributing the power of the priesthood. The priesthood does not have the strength that it should have."9 When we learn to set aside the things of the world and lead with love, we begin to connect with heaven and have *power* in the priesthood.

To lead with love is just as important in the home as it is in the Church. When you have a spouse and children, how will you treat them? This is the ultimate leadership position and one in which the Lord will hold us accountable. My wife and I walked into the sealing room of the South Carolina Temple many years ago. Before we entered the room, the sealer looked into our eyes and asked us each the question, "How do you treat each other?" and then he asked, "Do you love your partner and treat them with respect?" I had a strong impression that one of our initial meetings with Christ will be very similar, except that the full truth will be in front of us. He will be more concerned about our relationships and our ability to lead with love rather than our titles or positions.

The Lord can use you, as a returned missionary, to serve and bless the lives of many people if you lead with love, patience, and long-suffering. Beware of unrighteous dominion and compulsion. As you do, the Lord will draw near unto you and your light will grow brighter and brighter until the perfect day!

In a Nutshell

1. The Lord can utilize you to accomplish His purposes. He needs leaders who have charity and compassion. He needs leaders who set an example and teach by the Spirit.

2. If you are called to a leadership position, you have a solemn responsibility to be humble, seek the guidance of the Lord, and lead with love. If you don't, you will be accountable to Him.

3. In many cases, we need to realize that when a leader is called, they are on trial and that this may be *their* test. D&C 121:39 says, "We have learned by sad experience that it is the nature and disposition *of almost all* men, as soon as they get a little authority, as they suppose, *they will immediately begin to exercise unrighteous dominion*" (emphasis added).

4. It's possible to have authority but no power. A leader or priesthood holder receives power only when they connect with heaven and follow the counsel in D&C section 121.

5. President Uchtdorf wisely said, "In spite of this shining example, we too easily and too often get caught up in seeking the honors of men rather than serving the Lord with all our might, mind, and strength. The Lord judges so very differently from the way we do. He is pleased with the noble servant, not with the self-serving noble."

6. When we learn to set aside the things of the world and lead with love, then we begin to connect with heaven and have *power* in the priesthood.

CHAPTER 10
Understand the Difference between the Church and the Gospel

"And it came to pass that thus they [His disciples] did go forth among all the people of Nephi, and did preach the gospel of Christ unto all people upon the face of the land; and they were converted unto the Lord, and were united unto the church of Christ, and thus the people of that generation were blessed."
(3 Nephi 28:23)

THERE ARE MANY PEOPLE WHO return from their missions and, within a short amount of time, lose their testimonies and love of the gospel. Even though it has blessed their lives, they withdraw themselves from the Church and start doing things I don't think they ever expected to be doing. The number of returned missionaries who go inactive or leave the Church is far too high. You might be tempted to say, "Well, it can never happen to me." I cannot count how many people I have heard say those very words—and then it happens to them.

In addition to everything else we talk about in this book that will help you succeed, this is one area that needs to be discussed because it will be critical to your success in the gospel and it is one of the reasons so many people I know have left the Church.

For some reason, we as humans will often subconsciously apply a standard of worthiness or accomplishment to a position or calling.

For example, person X is a member of the Seventy or Twelve, and therefore, by virtue of the calling, what he says is always right. It happens in business and government as well. It is common in Western culture. We (unfairly to the person with a calling) tend to subconsciously put a person with a "higher" calling on a pedestal, forgetting they are human just like we are and that they will make mistakes just like anyone else.

When someone is offended, they periodically attribute the offense to the Church or a leader (or mistakenly the gospel) and walk away. If someone does or says something offensive, that person is not the Church. How many people did you meet on your mission who were inactive because they were offended? We know that leaders are not perfect, and just because a current or former leader shared an opinion or said something incorrect doesn't mean the gospel isn't true. It's critical to separate the Church and its members from the eternal gospel.

In the April 2012 general conference, Elder Donald Hallstrom gave a talk titled "Converted to His Gospel through His Church."

Elder Hallstrom said, "I love the gospel of Jesus Christ *and* The Church of Jesus Christ of Latter-day Saints. Sometimes we use the terms *gospel* and *Church* interchangeably, but they are not the same. They are, however, exquisitely interconnected, and we need both."[10]

Why is it important to understand this concept as a returned missionary? One reason is to safeguard and grow your testimony and relationship with Christ. Once we understand that the gospel and the Church are both extremely important, but separate, we can move forward with confidence.

I know many people who have lost their testimony because they cannot separate the two. For example, some may find statements from previous Church leaders that contradict statements from other leaders, or they find a piece of Church history that does not sit well with them. I've heard members teach that the Church is perfect, and when they teach that, they paint themselves into a corner. When they find a flaw in the Church, its history, or one of its leaders, many lose their testimony or have it seriously shaken.

The Church leaders are going to great lengths to discuss points of Church history that may not be pretty, and they are getting the truth out there for people to see. We are all human, so we all make mistakes. We should not hold any leader to a standard of perfection or infallibility. There was only one infallible person: Jesus Christ!

The Church is an incredible vehicle when it comes to such astounding accomplishments as printing and publishing the Book of Mormon, building temples and places of worship where ordinances can be administered, and providing a missionary force of tens of thousands of missionaries. However, the Church is not the gospel; they are intertwined with each other but still separate. One is imperfect and one is perfect. The gospel is how we internalize and live eternal truths; the Church is the vehicle that delivers them to us.

Consider another excerpt from Elder Hallstrom's address:

> Some have come to think of activity in the Church as the ultimate goal. Therein lies a danger. It is possible to be active in the Church and less active in the gospel. Let me stress: activity in the Church is a highly desirable goal; however, it is insufficient. Activity in the Church is an outward indication of our spiritual desire. If we attend our meetings, hold and fulfill Church responsibilities, and serve others, it is publicly observed.
>
> By contrast, the things of the gospel are usually less visible and more difficult to measure, but they are of greater eternal importance. For example, how much faith do we really have? How repentant are we? How meaningful are the ordinances in our lives? How focused are we on our covenants?
>
> I repeat: we need the gospel *and* the Church. In fact, the purpose of the Church is to help

us live the gospel. We often wonder: How can someone be fully active in the Church as a youth and then not be when they are older? How can an adult who has regularly attended and served stop coming? How can a person who was disappointed by a leader or another member allow that to end their Church participation? Perhaps the reason is they were not sufficiently converted to the gospel—the things of eternity.

This is the main point for writing this chapter. Although activity in the Church is very important, it is not the end goal. It is not about how "high we go" or what callings we have held. The endowment teaches that the real end goal is to pass through the veil and return to the presence of the Lord. The Church is very important in helping us get there. As a returned missionary, the Lord needs you to be active in both His Church and His gospel. It's not about the white shirt and tie or the nice dress if we are totally different people throughout the rest of the week.

Consider it this way: The Church is the vehicle to deliver the principles and ordinances of the gospel. The gospel is about our relationship with Christ and how we internalize and live those principles. Thus we come to know Him by strict obedience to Him and by loving service to others. If we receive the important parts of the gospel through the Church but we don't internalize and live them, they become meaningless in our individual progression.

As a returned missionary, don't let imperfect leaders in the Church or an imperfect history of the Church shake your testimony of the perfect gospel. For almost two centuries, imperfect people have tried to deliver the gospel to the people of the earth. Sometimes leaders have stumbled and mistakes have been made, but the Lord will find and lift those who receive the gospel through the vehicle of the Church.

Joseph Smith shared great advice regarding how to look at others, including our neighbors and leaders: "I do not dwell on your faults, and you shall not upon mine."[11] On another occasion, Joseph also said, "I charged the Saints not to follow the example of the adversary in accusing the brethren, and said, 'If you do not accuse each other, God will not accuse you. If you have no accuser you will enter heaven, and if you will follow the revelations and instructions which God gives you through me, I will take you into heaven as my back load. If you will not accuse me, I will not accuse you. If you will throw a cloak of charity over my sins, I will over yours—for charity covereth a multitude of sins.'"12

We also read in the Book of Mormon:

> Verily, verily, I say unto you, Judge not, that ye be not judged. For with what judgement ye judge, ye shall be judged; and with what measure ye mete, it shall be measured to you again. And why beholdest thou the mote that is in thy brother's eye, but considerest not the beam that is in thine own eye? Or how wilt thou say to thy brother: Let me pull the mote out of thine eye—and behold, a beam is in thine own eye? Thou hypocrite, first cast the beam out of thine own eye; and then shalt thou see clearly to cast the mote out of thy brother's eye. (3 Nephi 14:1–5)

I am a strong advocate of searching for the truth and understanding our history. However, please be careful to distinguish truth from error. Just because it is on the Internet does not make it truthful. Use charity when judging the mistakes of others, both past and present, for the same measure with which you judge, you will be judged. If you find something that doesn't seem to fit, avoid getting so hung up on that one point that you lose sight of everything else. Remember, all truth is circumscribed into one great whole.

The Church and the Lord need you to carry forth the gospel to the world. No, the Church does not have a perfect past, but it plays a vital role in spreading the truth and providing essential ordinances that show us the way back to Christ. Despite our many imperfections as mortals and leaders, I love the good the Church has done throughout the world as it spreads the gospel message. I believe the Church and kingdom of God will continue to roll forth until it fills the earth in preparation for the return of the Savior. The easy road is to nitpick and criticize; the high road is to look for the positive and serve others. There will continue to be challenges, but you can be a part of the solution and the answer!

IN A NUTSHELL

1. We (unfairly to the person with a calling) tend to subconsciously put a person with a "higher" calling on a pedestal, forgetting that they are human just like we are and that they will make mistakes just like anyone else.

2. Understanding the difference between the Church and the gospel may make all the difference in preserving and strengthening our testimonies.

3. Elder Donald Hallstrom said, "I love the gospel of Jesus Christ *and* The Church of Jesus Christ of Latter-day Saints. Sometimes we use the terms *gospel* and *Church* interchangeably, but they are not the same. They are, however, exquisitely interconnected, and we need both. . . . Some have come to think of activity in the Church as the ultimate goal. Therein lies a danger. It is possible to be active in the Church and less active in the gospel."

4. Some have taught that the Church is perfect, and then when they find a flaw in the Church or one of its leaders, they lose their testimony or at least have it seriously shaken.

5. We should not hold any leader to a standard of perfection or infallibility. There was only one infallible person: Jesus Christ!

6. The Church is an incredible vehicle when it comes to printing the Book of Mormon, building temples where ordinances can be administered, and providing a missionary force of tens of thousands of missionaries. However, the Church is not the gospel; they are intertwined with each other but still separate. One is imperfect, and one is perfect.

CHAPTER 11
Continue to Learn through Balanced Studies

"And as all have not faith, seek ye diligently and teach one another words of wisdom; yea, seek ye out of the best books words of wisdom; seek learning, even by study and also by faith."
(D&C 88:118)

IT'S NOT JUST A SUGGESTION to read, study, and ponder. The Lord has commanded it.

Have you ever climbed a mountain and enjoyed the amazing views at the summit? Gaining knowledge through study and prayer is similar. When you start climbing from the valley floor, you typically cannot see much of the landscape or features around you. Then, as you begin to ascend the mountain, entirely new vistas appear. You might be able to see how a river winds its way through the valley or begin to see lakes or ponds that weren't visible before. As you continue to ascend, sometimes the views are so amazing that you might stop to take pictures, not realizing that even more incredible vistas are just ahead. Finally, after a great deal of effort, you near the peak and an incredible panoramic view of the entire surrounding area emerges. Sometimes you can look down on the clouds below, which are nestled on the valley floor like large cotton balls. It's an incredible moment as you take in the breathtaking scene that lies before you.

Gaining knowledge is similar. We may think we understand a certain doctrine or principle, and then as we continue to study, our knowledge on the subject opens up new and beautiful vistas.

Here is one example. Moses was already chosen by the Lord as a prophet and had a fairly strong understanding of the gospel. However, look carefully at the following experience and how he describes it in Moses 1:7–10: "And now, behold, this one thing I show unto thee, Moses, my son, for thou art in the world, and now I show it unto thee. And it came to pass that Moses looked, and beheld the world upon which he was created; and Moses beheld the world and the ends thereof, and all the children of men which are, and which were created; of the same he greatly marveled and wondered. And the presence of God withdrew from Moses, that his glory was not upon Moses; and Moses was left unto himself. And as he was left unto himself, he fell unto the earth. And it came to pass that it was for the space of many hours before Moses did again receive his natural strength like unto man; and he said unto himself: Now, for this cause I know that man is nothing, which thing I never had supposed."

Moses, already a prophet, learned something so vast and amazing that he astonishingly proclaimed, "Now I know that man is nothing, which thing I never had supposed." Here is a great lesson for us. We may think we understand something, but there is so much more waiting if we will search and study through diligent effort and prayer. We will gain so much more by being open-minded, realizing we understand so little about the things of eternity, rather than being closed-minded in the thought that we've "got it."

Think about this: Joseph Smith said, "A man is saved no faster than he gets knowledge, for if he does not get knowledge, he will be brought into captivity by some evil power in the other world."[13]

On another occasion, Joseph was speaking from the pulpit when he turned to his Apostles sitting behind him (including John Taylor, Brigham Young, and Parley Pratt) and exclaimed, "'Brethren, if I were to tell you all I know of the kingdom of God, I do know that you would rise up and kill me.' Brother Brigham arose and said, 'Don't tell me anything that I can't bear, for I don't want to apostatize.'"14 This should remind us that there is so much more to the gospel and that we have only scraped the surface. Why would his closest friends, the Apostles of the Restoration, rise up and kill him if he were to share all he knew? One reason may be that the older we get, the more our own opinions become our own reality and we tend to close our minds to new ideas that don't match our opinions.

If we study and learn with an open mind, the Lord can reach out and teach us amazing things. Remember the Pharisees, who couldn't be taught because their minds were closed and they thought they had it all figured out. Let us be more like Nephi, Peter, and others who humbly studied and learned.

In D&C 130:18–19, we are taught, "Whatever principle of intelligence we attain unto in this life, it will rise with us in the resurrection. And if a person gains more knowledge and intelligence in this life through his diligence and obedience than another, he will have so much the advantage in the world to come." Knowledge comes through diligence and obedience. As you study and learn (and obey), the Lord will enlighten your mind according to His time and will.

Let me offer a few ideas or suggestions that have helped me and many others grow and stay centered on the gospel through effective study habits. Some of these ideas might be helpful to you as well:

- **Read often and balance your studies.** If you find yourself spending a significant amount of time on a single website, forum, or chat group, use caution. This can stimulate great conversation, but if you don't discern carefully, it has the potential to skew your thinking and get you hyperfocused in one area. I know quite a few people who have lost their testimonies because they began focusing on a single point of doctrine that bothered them and they lost the big picture. A balanced study helps us stay open-minded versus a hyperfocused study, which leads to being narrow-minded.

Give yourself equal time in different areas of the gospel, and never neglect your study of the scriptures. As mentioned previously, a possible red flag might be if you find yourself always going to a single website or forum to get your information. Remember the counsel in the D&C to study from the best books. Some of those books include books General Authorities have written as well as a host of other inspired authors. There are many authors who can share great insights about different parts of the gospel. Learn from the best books.

About seven years ago, I read a life-changing piece of advice. The advice was to read at least one book a month. The more I travel, the more it becomes apparent that successful leaders are readers. If you want to earn more, then learn more. This includes books both about the gospel and about other topics such as leadership, motivation, how to be a better parent or spouse, how to improve at your job, and special areas of interest such as travel, history, or science. The mind is like a muscle. What happens if a person sits on a couch all day long every day of the week? Their muscles atrophy! The mind is no different, and reading unlocks a part of the brain that would otherwise stay dormant. Reading is a way to exercise and stimulate your mind, and it is a powerful habit of success.

You can learn from the Internet, podcasts, and books. What I'm suggesting here is that it is important to actually read often, whether that happens on an e-reader or in a physical book.

If this is already an ingrained habit, great. If not, I invite you to come up with a list of at least six books to get you through the next six months. If you're not sure where to start, try asking a mentor which books he or she would suggest; you could also go to book-selling websites and search for "motivation," "leadership," or any subject you want to research more in depth. If you use the Internet for this search, read the customer reviews and book description to make sure the book looks interesting to you and has appropriate content.

Use the space below to write your list of the next six books you want to read:

The number-one piece of advice I can offer regarding a balanced study and what you read is to always give equal time to the scriptures. If you spend thirty minutes on a website, forum, or in other books, then invest thirty minutes in the scriptures as well.

- **Ask questions and look for answers.** Cecil Samuelson gave a great talk at a BYU devotional on November 13, 2001, titled "The Importance of Asking Questions." He wisely taught, "Some seem to believe that faith and questions are antithetical. Such could not be further from the truth. The Restoration itself was unfolded by the proper and necessary melding of both. The Prophet Joseph Smith had both faith and questions. Indeed, the passage of scripture that led Joseph to the Sacred Grove experience includes both a question and the promise of an answer based on the asker's faith."[15]

  He goes on to make a great point as he quotes Joseph Smith: "'In the midst of this war of words and tumult of opinions, I often said to myself [Joseph Smith]: What is to be done? Who of all these parties are right; or, are they all wrong together? If any one of them be right, which is it, and how shall I know it?' [JS–H 1:10].

  "I would submit to you that these three questions constitute much more than Joseph's passive curiosity. They allowed him to focus on resolving his own personal dilemma and also prepared him to have that experience so critical to the lives of all of us."

Asking the right questions sets the stage for answers, both from a dedicated study and through personal revelation. Joseph asked many questions, and he learned to expect answers from the Lord, even if they were not the answers he anticipated.

I invite you to take out a piece of paper and write down some key questions you have about the gospel. Then make a study plan to learn and seek answers to those questions. Something that can make all the difference in the world is to involve fasting and prayer. Before you study, invite the Spirit to help you discern truth from error. Oftentimes people wonder why the heavens seem closed to them. When you ask specific questions and put in the effort to seek answers, revelation will eventually come. The Lord will reward your effort.

- **Be patient.** Sometimes we want answers and we want them on our time line. We want to rush the Lord into giving us the answers now. If you prayerfully and sincerely seek answers to your questions through study and effort, the answers will come. However, it may take a lot longer than you expect to get the answers to some of your questions—some answers may not come until later in life. Trust the Lord and His timing. Looking back on your own life so far, aren't you glad you did not get certain answers until you were mature enough to appreciate and understand them? Aren't you glad that some prayers went unanswered, or at least that's how it felt at the time?

  Always remember we are to learn line upon line, precept upon precept. The Lord can teach you and periodically reveal great truths in a wonderful manifestation (as with Nephi and Moses), but we all need to be patient with Him and remember He knows the right time to reveal certain truths to each of us.

- **Prayerfully read the conference edition of the *Ensign* and pray for two action items per talk.** Elder Craig Zwick was at a stake conference in St. Petersburg, Florida. During his talk, he invited all of the members to prayerfully read the entire conference edition of the *Ensign* and find two "action items" per talk. That was great advice.

This approach opens the windows of revelation. It is not so much what you read or what was said during the talk, it is what the Spirit invites you to do as a result of reading it. You may feel a prompting to do something that has nothing to do with what you are reading. By reading and pondering those talks, you put yourself in an environment to receive personal revelation. As a reminder, one of the keys is to always start your study with a sincere prayer.

I took Elder Zwick up on his challenge and read the conference edition of the *Ensign* with the intent of finding two action items per talk as directed by the Spirit. Pretty soon I had a strong list of things I could do for myself and others. Some of those included visiting a certain widow, spending more quality time with my children, and reading my patriarchal blessing.

This is part of a balanced study of the gospel. In addition to books and scriptures, we should carefully study talks from general conference and seek personal revelation.

- **Keep a thoughts and life-events journal.** When you have questions, write them down. When you get answers or new ideas, write them down. Not only will this help increase revelation while studying, you can go back and review some of your lessons learned and personal insights. If you keep up this habit, you'll look back in five or ten years and be amazed at what you wrote. Elder Richard G. Scott offers the wise counsel that the act of writing mentally engages parts of your brain that otherwise remain dormant. Writing and taking notes is an act of participation.

  You should also keep track of important life events. I recently sat down with my teenage son and read some of my mission journal entries from many years earlier. I was amazed at how many stories had vanished from my memory until we went back and read them together. Had they not been written down, they would be gone forever. One way to help with this is to set aside a certain time every Sunday and record the highlights from your week. Aren't you grateful you kept a journal on your mission? You will be equally grateful to have a record of this time in your life.

- **Study your patriarchal blessing often.** When you prayerfully study your patriarchal blessing, it can help you find answers. Read it often. Pray about its meaning. Ponder the words and ask the Lord to provide you light and direction regarding your blessing. This is a prophetic statement about your future, and the length of your blessing is irrelevant. I suggest that a person study and ponder their patriarchal blessing at least once a month, if not more often.

   Reading it often is a great start, and even better, memorize your patriarchal blessing. If you're feeling up to the challenge, I invite you to memorize your blessing in the next sixty days.

I hear some people say "focus on the basics" to excuse a further and deeper study of the gospel. While I understand the premise of that statement, to ignore the importance of gaining deeper knowledge of the gospel is a great error. If Moses, Abraham, Nephi, Alma, Joseph Smith, and many others had not studied, labored intensively to learn and grow, and earnestly prayed, they may never have had the wonderful experiences they had.

D&C 131:6 clearly teaches, "It is impossible for a man to be saved in ignorance."

As a returned missionary, you have the opportunity to take all of your experience, knowledge, and lessons learned and use them as a springboard. Hopefully you had some incredible experiences while studying, and now you can continue to ascend on that path of faith and knowledge. The Lord will reveal great things as you put in the effort and sacrifice to learn the mysteries of eternity. Please remember to be open-minded, always realizing that we've barely scraped the surface.

A balanced study of the gospel can unlock amazing truths and help you become an effective instrument in the hands of the Lord. He will reward your efforts, study, and sacrifice.

In a Nutshell

1. We may think we understand a certain doctrine or principle, and then as we continue to study, our knowledge on the subject opens up new and beautiful vistas. Think about Moses, who already had a great understanding of the gospel. After the Lord showed him His creations, Moses said, "Now, for this cause I know that man is nothing, which thing I never had supposed."

2. "A man is saved no faster than he gets knowledge, for if he does not get knowledge, he will be brought into captivity by some evil power in the other world."16

3. **Read often and balance your studies.** Be careful about spending too much time on a single website, forum, or chat group. Make the scriptures a central focus of your study.

4. **Ask questions and look for answers.** Cecil Samuelson wisely taught, "Some seem to believe that faith and questions are antithetical. Such could not be further from the truth. The Restoration itself was unfolded by the proper and necessary melding of both. The Prophet Joseph Smith had both faith and questions."

5. **Prayerfully read the conference *Ensign* and pray for two action items per talk.** It is not so much what was said, it is what the Spirit invites you to do as a result of reading it.

6. **Keep a thoughts and life-events journal.** When you have questions, write them down. When you get answers or new ideas, write them down. One of the habits of successful people throughout history includes keeping a journal and recording their thoughts.

7. **Study your patriarchal blessing often.** Read it often. Pray about its meaning. Ponder it and ask the Lord to provide you light and direction regarding your blessing.

CHAPTER 12
Final Tips for Success

"And we began to till the ground, yea, even with all manner of seeds, with seeds of corn, and of wheat, and of barley, and with neas, and with sheum, and with seeds of all manner of fruits; and we did begin to multiply and prosper in the land."
(Mosiah 9:9)

EARLY IN MY FIGHTER PILOT career, a senior leader gave me some sage advice. His wise counsel was, "Open as many doors as possible, and you be the one to close them rather than have someone close the door for you." This means that when you put yourself in a position where you have multiple options and opportunities, then you are the one who gets to choose your course, rather than someone else making the choice for you.

As a returned missionary, you are in a great position to open doors. You stand at the threshold of life, where you get to decide what career to pursue, whom to marry, and where to live. The decisions you make in the first three to five years after your mission will determine a significant portion of your future.

In this final chapter, I'll share several things you can do to open doors for yourself and put yourself in a position to succeed in life. Let's take a look:

- **Have a great attitude!** Think about and ponder the following quotes and how they apply to you:

    "Success starts with attitude!" James Malinchak (businessman and public speaker)

    "As a man thinketh, so is he." James Allen (British philosophical writer)

    "Ability is what you're capable of doing. Motivation determines what you do. Attitude determines how well you do it." Lou Holtz (*ESPN*'s doctor of football and life philosophy)

    "Everything can be taken from a man but one thing: the last of human freedoms—to choose one's attitude in any given set of circumstances, to choose one's own way." Viktor Frankl (Austrian neurologist and psychiatrist; holocaust survivor)

    "Your attitude, not your aptitude, will determine your altitude." Zig Ziglar (American author, salesman, and motivational speaker)

    So much of your success depends on your attitude. Have you ever been around an "energy sucker," someone who is negative and complains all day? How does it feel to be around that type of person?

    Conversely, have you been around someone who is genuinely positive, uplifting, and complimentary? How does that feel? Which person do you want to be?

    A friend of mine wrote a book in which he describes how changing the way we look at a situation can immediately change our attitude. For example, my brother-in-law was on a flight one month ago. Behind him sat a parent who spent two hours wrestling with a screaming baby and kicking his chair. At first my brother-in-law was upset and irritated, but then he decided to change the way he looked at the situation and express gratitude instead of frustration. He thought to himself how grateful he was to have ears to hear the crying baby. He wondered how many people in the world would love to be able to hear that baby. That's how powerfully gratitude can affect our attitude!

Find a way to make lemonade out of lemons. Be the person who is positive and uplifting when others choose not to be. No matter how difficult your situation, find a way to focus on the positive, and this will open countless doors. Most people want to be around someone who makes them feel good, so have a great attitude and be positive about life.

- **Get an education.** Statistically, the more education you have, the more opportunities you will have. When you interview for a job, you will quickly discover that businesses may eliminate you from the job pool simply because you don't have a bachelor's or master's degree.

Can you do extremely well without a college degree? Absolutely! However, in most cases, the higher your level of education, the more opportunities you will have. Look at the following graph from the 2010 U.S. Census as it relates to median income versus education level:

Median Incomes Vary Greatly by Educational Attainment

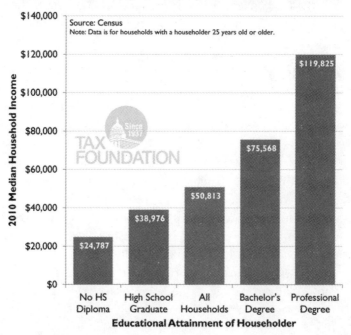

Source: Census
Note: Data is for households with a householder 25 years old or older.

No doubt college is an expensive investment. I've heard a lot of reasons why people cannot get an education. At the same time, I've met people who came from the poorest of backgrounds with no support from their parents and they found a way to complete their degrees. If you want it badly enough, you can make it happen. If finances are the challenge, then here are a few ideas to use:

Get an additional part-time job.

Apply for a Pell grant or scholarship.

Attend an in-state institution.

Consider joining an ROTC program at the university.

Begin at a two-year college, where tuition is typically lower.

Eliminate unnecessary expenses in your life. For example, how important is cable TV, a nice car, eating out often, or big data plans for your phone?

Avoid the temptation to postpone your education. It almost always becomes more difficult with time, since the demands on your time will only increase as you get older.

Remember, education will open doors for you, and then you get to be the one to close those doors at your choosing.

- **Ask for at least one blessing per year.** A tradition that started in our family when I was just a boy was to gather around prior to school and get a father's blessing. I still remember those special experiences when my father laid his hands on my head to give me a blessing. In my case, I've been fortunate to be able to ask my father for additional blessings throughout my life.

Unfortunately, many of us grow up and become stubborn. Many of us are reluctant to ask for blessings. I invite and encourage you to seek out a blessing at least one time each year. If your father is in a position to give the blessing, seek that blessing from him in the patriarchal tradition. However, I realize that many people don't have a father or a close relative to call on. In those cases, you can ask a worthy priesthood holder whom you know and who is close to the Spirit. Maybe that is a friend, a home teacher, a former companion, or your bishop.

A couple of years ago, I was in a high priest group meeting and I asked how many of those men (whose fathers were still alive) had asked their father for a blessing in the past few years. Only one hand went up. In my opinion, the men in that room had missed some great opportunities.

Prior to his death, Adam gathered his posterity and blessed them. Lehi did the same with his family. Not only is this an opportunity for a father to exercise the priesthood in the patriarchal role, it is a powerful bonding experience between father and son or daughter.

This will be a wonderful experience in your life. To make it easier, choose a time of year such as the start of a school year or the beginning of the year and then simply make it a tradition. Start this tradition with your own children as well.

- **Apply to many jobs and universities.** When you apply to a university, apply to several different universities, even if you don't think you have much of a chance. If they all say yes, then YOU get to choose which university to attend. Even if two of them say yes, you still have the choice.

  If you apply for a job, apply for a bunch of different jobs that excite and motivate you. If you apply for thirty different jobs, you may have six of them respond with interest. Now you are in a position to choose the one you think is best and most exciting to you rather than just depending on a response from one or two.

  The point is to apply often and give yourself choices. As I mentioned earlier, this is all about opening as many doors as possible. Then you get to choose which doors to close.

- **Meet others who have been successful doing what you want to do.** Find someone who has been successful doing what you want to do and offer to take them to lunch or dinner. You may have one or two grumpy people who refuse, but almost everyone I know would make time if someone invited them to a meal. If they ask you why you want to go to lunch,

your response is, "Because you have been very successful at
what you have done and I am just starting out. I would be
so grateful if you would allow me to ask you a few questions
and maybe learn from some of the lessons you have learned. I
would greatly appreciate any time you might be able to make
for a few questions." If you approach it like that, you will find
a positive response almost every time. Most people want to
help, but very few people actually ask them for advice. Find
someone who has been successful and learn what helped with
their success. Always remember that success leaves clues and
you'll find those clues when you learn from people who have
already walked the path. If possible, make this person part
of your mastermind group or another network. You will be
amazed how many doors open up because of who you know
or someone you have met along the way.

- **Treat others kindly.** You never know who may come back
  and help you. I know someone who called a CEO and treated
  the executive assistant poorly—costly mistake! The executive
  assistant told the CEO that this person treated her rudely, and
  the CEO told her to never return his call again. He wanted
  nothing to do with a person who treated his assistant poorly.

  In another example, I know a person who treated someone kindly who seemingly had nothing to offer. Little did the
  kind person know that this would lead to a huge business
  opportunity. The person who seemingly had nothing to offer
  was the cousin of a very successful business person. She connected the kind person to her successful cousin, and a profit-
  able relationship was born.

  Always treat people kindly and with respect because you
  never know how your paths may cross again in the future.
  Whether in business or in day-to-day living, the way you
  treat others now will be a reflection of your success in life.

- **Create a plan using MyPlan.lds.org.** This is a great resource
  to help you develop a plan after your mission. If you haven't

seen or heard of this page, put down this book and check it out now.

It will walk you through some of the key areas to think about if you want to maintain a strong testimony and be successful both in the gospel and in life.

These are just a few things you can do right now to open doors and be successful throughout your life. The idea is to open as many doors as possible and then close them when you are ready. It doesn't matter your background, race, or gender; you can be successful if you have the faith and put in the required effort to open doors that would otherwise remain closed.

In a Nutshell

1. *Open as many doors as possible and you be the one to close them rather than have someone close the door for you.* Do the things that will give you multiple options so you are the one who gets to choose, rather than letting someone else make the choice for you.

2. **Have a great attitude!** So much of your success depends on your attitude. Find a way to make lemonade out of lemons. Be positive when others choose not to be. Remember what James Allen said: "As a man thinketh, so is he."

3. **Get an education.** Statistically, the more education you have, the more opportunities you will have. Avoid the temptation to postpone your education.

4. **Ask for at least one blessing per year.** Many of us are reluctant to ask for blessings. I invite you to be humble and seek out a blessing at least one time each year.

5. **Apply to many jobs and universities.** Apply often and give yourself choices. Open as many doors as possible so you get to choose which doors to close.

6. **Meet others who have been successful doing what you want to do.** Offer to take them to lunch and ask them to share their lessons learned. Learn from their experience!

7. **Treat people kindly.** Always treat people kindly and with respect because you never know how your paths may cross again in the future.

8. **Create a plan using MyPlan.lds.org.** This is a great resource to help you develop a plan after your mission. If you haven't seen or heard of this page, check it out right now.

CONCLUSION

It doesn't matter whether you served as a sister or an elder. It doesn't matter what callings you have had. It doesn't matter whether you finished your mission or returned early for whatever reason.

Your future is in front of you, and the majority of your time should be used looking forward. Learn important lessons from your past, then move on. If you have done things you regret, then repent, learn the lessons, and look forward to the future with an eye of faith.

It is said that when you are running toward the horizon, it doesn't feel like you are getting any closer or making any progress. It is not until you look over your shoulder that you see how far you have actually gone. Life is similar; it may not feel like you are making much progress, but keep running and eventually you will look over your shoulder and be amazed at how far you have come.

As we finish this book, let me share a few inspiring quotes to consider as you go forward:

President Gordon B. Hinckley: "Generally speaking, the most miserable people I know are those who are obsessed with themselves; the happiest people I know are those who lose themselves in the service of others. . . . By and large, I have come to see that if we complain about life, it is because we are thinking only of ourselves."[17]

President Spencer W. Kimball: "Jesus said several times, 'Come, follow me.' His was a program of 'do what I do,' rather than 'do what I say.' His innate brilliance would have permitted him to put on a dazzling display, but that would have left his followers far behind. He walked and worked with those he was to serve. His was not a long-distance leadership. He was not afraid of close friendships; he was not afraid that proximity to him would disappoint his followers. The leaven of true leadership cannot lift others unless we are with and serve those to be led."[18]

President Gordon B. Hinckley: "The best antidote I know for worry is work. . . . The best cure for weariness is the challenge of helping someone who is even more tired. . . . One of the great ironies of life is this: He or she who serves almost always benefits more than he or she who is served."[19]

Elder Neil L. Andersen: "Your mission will be a sacred opportunity to bring others to Christ and help prepare for the Second Coming of the Savior."[20]

I know that Christ is real and that He lives. He is not some distant person. He, along with His angels, continues to minister to the people of this earth regardless of calling, race, or gender. The windows of heaven are open. You and I have a sacred calling to prepare the world for His return. We talk about the "last days," but there will be a "last day." Search for Him in this life, learn of Him, and continue to develop your relationship with Him so that you can rejoice and kneel at His feet in the not-so-distant future.

When you return from your full-time missionary service, your true mission begins. You will likely become a spouse, and you may be given the sacred responsibility of raising children unto the Lord.

Your life will be a marathon, not a sprint. Look back on where you've been and learn the lessons from your past, but turn your eyes to the future. You have an enormous amount of potential, and the Lord can use you for incredible good in this world. Good luck in your journey!

BIBLIOGRAPHY

1 Bruce R. McConkie, "The Rock of Salvation," Conference Report, Oct. 1969.

2 Bruce R. McConkie, *The Promised Messiah* (Salt Lake City: Deseret Book, 1981), 583.

3 Nolan P. Olsen, *Logan Temple: The First 100 Years* (Logan: Watkins Printing, 1978).

4 Henry B. Eyring, "Serve with the Spirit," *Ensign*, Nov. 2010.

5 Ezra Taft Benson, "To the 'Youth of the Noble Birthright,'" *Ensign*, May 1986.

6 Spencer W. Kimball, "Boys Need Heroes Close By," *Ensign*, May 1976.

7 Gail Matthews, "Study Backs up Strategies for Achieving Goals," Dominican University of California, n.d. Web. 6 December 2013.

8 Dieter F. Uchtdorf, "Lift Where You Stand," *Ensign*, Nov. 2008.

9 Body K. Packer, "The Power of the Priesthood," *Ensign,* May 2010.

10 Donald Hallstrom, "Converted to His Gospel through His Church," *Ensign*, May 2012.

11 Joseph Smith, *History of the Church of Jesus Christ of Latter-day Saints*, vol. 5, 517.

12 Joseph Smith, *Teachings of the Prophet Joseph Smith* (Salt Lake City: Deseret Book, 1976), 193.

13 Joseph Smith, *Teachings of the Prophet Joseph Smith,* 217.

14 *The Latter-Day Saints' Millennial Star*, vol. 55, 585.

15 Cecil O. Samuelson, "The Importance of Asking Questions," BYU Devotional, Nov. 13, 2001.

16 Joseph Smith, *Teachings of the Prophet Joseph Smith*, 217.

17 Gordon B. Hinckley, "Whosoever Will Save His Life," *Ensign*, Aug. 1982.

18 Spencer W. Kimball, "Jesus: The Perfect Leader," YPO address in Sun Valley, Aug. 1979.

19 Gordon B. Hinckley, *Teachings of Gordon B. Hinckley* (Salt Lake City: Deseret Book, 1997), 595–596.

20 Neil L. Andersen, "Preparing the World for the Second Coming," *Ensign*, Apr. 2011.